STORIES & SHADOWS

from

Salem's

P A S T

Keep the music in the air & in your heart. Blessings,

Maggi

Winter 2011

STORIES & SHADOWS

from

Salem's

PAST

NAUMKEAG NOTATIONS

MAGGI SMITH-DALTON

Charleston · London

THE
History
PRESS

Published by The History Press
Charleston, SC 29403
www.historypress.net

Front cover: Illustration by F.T. Merrill in Samuel Adams Drake's *A Book of New England's Legends and Folk Lore in Prose and Poetry.* Back cover: *Courtesy of the author.*

First published 2010

Manufactured in the United States

ISBN 978.1.60949.017.1

Library of Congress Cataloging-in-Publication Data

Smith-Dalton, Maggi.
Stories and shadows from Salem's past : Naumkeag notations / by Maggi Smith-Dalton.
p. cm.
Includes bibliographical references.
ISBN 978-1-60949-017-1
1. Salem (Mass.)--History--Anecdotes. 2. Salem (Mass.)--Social life and customs--Anecdotes. 3. Salem (Mass.)--Biography. I. Title.
F74.S1S64 2010
974.4'5--dc22
2010025317

This book is dedicated jointly to the memory of my father, Edward Joseph Smith, and to my wonderful husband, James B. Dalton.

Contents

Introduction

W hat could the meeting be about, I wondered?

It was early in the school year—not even my birthday yet—and here was a note from my teacher requesting a meeting with my parents. I couldn't think of anything to be especially worried about; well, I *did* have that wild crush on the tall, dark and handsome Mr. T. But, I suspected, it had more to do with the "she's too serious, too shy, too bookish" chorus I was already, by the fifth grade, learning to expect from my teachers. (I never did, and still don't, understand why shyness and a choice not to be a social butterfly was considered to be such a fault.)

When they came home, I couldn't read the looks on their faces. I suspect now, looking back on it, that they literally didn't know what to do. But the news they gave me when they sat me down to have a private talk was so wonderful and exciting that it soon became apparent that I had more reason to hug Mr. T. than any schoolgirl crush would warrant.

Mr. T., my dad said, explained to them that he could offer three choices for my educational future in the fifth grade. As had been suggested to my parents almost every year since I entered school, I could be skipped a grade or two ahead; I could go home for the rest of fifth grade and come back for sixth; or (and here, my dad and mom seemed stunned) I could continue to attend fifth grade and go to math class (ugh), gym (double ugh) and music; and then be dismissed for the rest of the day—to the library. (These were the days before the problematic institution of "gifted and talented" classes was invented.)

And so it was that every day I was allowed to wander—to wallow in—the wonderful world of books in our school library. I couldn't wait! Each day I paid the math and gym gods their pound of flesh and then hurried, breathless with delight, to the quiet room filled with books. I learned to read widely, deeply and with growing powers of discrimination. I read everything and supplemented it with my usual weekend trips to the town library or haunting the big brown bookmobile when it pulled into our little semisuburban enclave on the New Jersey shore. I had an insatiable curiosity; yet, it was history and nonfiction that sparked my intellectual loyalty. I dreamt of being a history teacher when I grew up.

When I was ten years old, it was discovered that I had serious musical talent and music became my life's purpose. Music claimed me for its own—an outlet for my passionate nature. (Yes, shy people *are* passionate!) Yet I have never forgotten my first love; as an adult I've been able to combine them: I became a professional musician at age eleven, and I began writing my first history, culture, and arts newspaper columns while still in my teens. It's been a long, happy journey since then.

So, Gentle Reader, here are some gleanings from recent columns that are reconstituted as chapters in a book about the historic, startling and often bemusing Salem, Massachusetts, where I landed some seven years ago. Written for the *Salem Gazette*, a newspaper revived in 2005 as a deliberate celebration of one of the most important newspapers in our regional—and national—history, these Naumkeag Notations wander and wallow in the multifaceted "stories and shadows" of my hometown. (Salem was originally named Naimcecke, Naumkeag or Naimkecke, which is the original Algonkian name for the harbor on which our maritime community would take root.)

I wish to earnestly thank all the folks who granted interviews, inspired curiosity, gave me advice and shared their research with me through these past few years. I especially thank my beloved husband and musical partner, Jim; my cherished colleague, historian Robert Booth; Bill Woolley and Lisa Guerriero, my editors at the *Salem Gazette*; and, of course, I thank my fifth-grade teacher, Mr. T., wherever he is!

Maggi Smith-Dalton, bookish musician and tuneful historian
Summer 2010

Chapter 1

People

"DISTINGUISHED FOR GENIUS"
MUSICAL MR. MCINTIRE

Architecture…is frozen music.
—*Friedrich von Schelling (1775–1854), the* Philosophy of Art

Architecture… [is] *silent music.*
—*Johann W. von Goethe (1749–1832)*

Congregation requested to rise during performance.
The following Lines sung as a Tribute of Respect to Mr. Samuel McIntire,
the Sunday after his Interment.
Few are our days—those few we dream away;
Sure is our fate to moulder in the clay.
Rise, immortal soul, above thine earthly fate;
Time yet is thine, but soon it is too late…
Rise, immortal soul, that hence thy fame may shine,
Time flies and ends, eternity is thine.
—*Manuscript in the collection of the Phillips Library, Peabody Essex Museum*

Where the Woodcarver of Salem now sleeps his eternal sleep, his memorial proclaims him "distinguished for Genius in Architecture, Sculpture and Musick: Modest and sweet Manners rendered him pleasing: Industry and Integrity respectable."

An eagle carved by Samuel McIntire, dated circa 1807, on a Salem mantelpiece. The author thanks Dean Lahikainen, Carolyn and Peter Lynch Curator of American Decorative Artt the Peabody Essex Museum, for his kind assistance in dating this work of art. *Courtesy of author.*

It is intriguing to note that architect and master carver Samuel McIntire was baptized in Salem in January 1757, the year in which a young George Washington began remodeling and enlarging his Mount Vernon home. Washington facilitated its restructuring from old into new, guided by his own talent for architecture. Washington was as conscious of the important statement his home made to the world as he was of his role in remodeling the political structure and identity of his native land.

When McIntire died in February 1811, he was lauded as a man "distinguished for Genius in Architecture, Sculpture, and Musick." He was also honored for his "virtuous Principles and unblemished conduct."

During that distinguished career in Salem, McIntire would be called upon to honor Washington, a man hailed as nearly godlike for his own "virtuous principles," with several artistic endeavors. Not the least important of these projects was his engagement by subscription for "ornamenting Washington Square," which was supported by donations of leading citizens of the town (a handwritten list dated May 20, 1802, in the Phillips Library, bears witness to this).[1] Part of the "ornamentation"

A list made on May 20, 1802, documented the contributions of many prominent citizens who supported the construction and design of the original gateway. Among donations of five, ten or twenty dollars, Samuel McIntire's name appears, offering "in carving" as his bit. *Courtesy of author.*

McIntire produced was a now-famous carved medallion portrait of President Washington.

As an architect and carver, his importance in the context of his time is well understood. Indeed, McIntire is credited—as scholar Fiske Kimball notes in his work, *Mr. Samuel McIntire, Carver: the Architect of Salem*[2]—with the restructuring and remodeling of his native town. "Salem at the end of his life presented a very different aspect from its appearance when he began his work…That was no idle phrase when the town clerk called Samuel McIntire…'the architect of Salem.'"

However, some of the most intriguing and apparently least-explored aspects of McIntire's life were his lifelong roles as a performer, teacher, and lover of music; and the reflections of post-Revolutionary- and Federal-period culture and society it provides. These aspects of his life are worthy of consideration because they offer a few surprises.

As noted recently in 2004's *Salem: Place, Myth, and Memory*, post-Revolutionary Salem "embraced innovation and enterprise"; in Robert Booth's engaging essay in that book, specific mention is made of the era's societal "cult of music," which defined a "smallish, powerful in-crowd in the new Salem—people with talent, taste, money and ambition…musical pursuits suddenly elevated a few members of the artisan class: Samuel McIntire…won acclaim as a violinist."[3]

Here's a picture of a young fun-loving set, which kicked their heels up, challenged the older standards of societal norms and erased certain social boundaries. During this period, wartime restrictions were lifted on theatrical amusements and other entertainments. It was a good time to be young and talented in America. McIntire's reported participation as a musician at parties and assemblies, however, was only one facet of understanding him as a man and as an artist.

That music was, as Kimball says, Samuel's "chief avocation" and extraordinarily important to him seems clear. That he was talented enough to have music married to architecture and sculpture in his final epitaph would seem to confirm how very seriously he took being a musician and how seriously others took him as a music maker. In the traces of his musical life that we can find, we glimpse a progressive and liberal mind, and yet concurrently—and perhaps seemingly paradoxically—a man who was aspiring to a more socially refined, orderly and educated expression of taste and accomplishment.

To get a better understanding of this, let's first listen to McIntire's friend and contemporary Dr. William Bentley, that diarist extraordinaire to whom we are all so indebted, as he commented on his own changing attitudes toward the uses and purposes of music in volumes one and two of his diary:

A Concert of music is proposed in St. Peter's Church to be on the evening following thanksgiving …The object is the repair of the Organ…The Band is to attend from Boston…it is singular that on a day of devotion we should be so weak as to be betrayed into a justification of an act against the practice of dissenters, not only to hear organs in a Church, but to go on thanksgiving day to pay for the repairs of one for the service. This is beyond Catholic. [1790]

We had no singing either in this morning or evening services…I regret that I shall be obliged to recant all I have against organs from mere necessity. [1791]

Sent & purchased at Boston a Bass Viol for 21 dollars. The fondness for Instrumental music in Churches so increases, that the inclination is not to be resisted. [1795]

Some efforts are making in this Town to create a love of Musick [sic]… *The hall is to be used on common occasions to teach Vocal musick.* [1798]

Thanksgiving Day…The fame of our Music attracted the notice of many persons, especially the young, & the house was unusually full. [1798]

The Several Societies in Salem have been induced to encourage Music from the introduction of an Organ into the Old Church. Macintire teaches for the North Church…Much is said of Mr. Holyoke's success at Newbury Port. [1801]

As we follow the good doctor through these permutations of attitude, we hear the echo of a rippling stream beginning its flow into a river of change. Now, let's look, in turn, at the evidence of Samuel McIntire's musical life. We can perhaps then begin to appreciate the direction in which that larger river flows and form a more complete picture of the context of his musical thinking.

In McIntire's estate at his death, as listed in the 1819 probate records, according to Kimball, were these items of interest:

> *a large Hand Organ with 10 barrels*
> *Vol.* Lock Hospital *(Music)*
> *Handel's* Messiah
> *a lot of Music Books*
> *a Double Bass (musical instrument)*
> *a Violin & case*
> *an Organ Chest*

Some of these items, with descriptions, were offered for sale in the April 30 and May 3, 1811 issues of the *Salem Gazette*:

> *1 elegant Barrel Organ, 6 feet high, 10 barrels*
> *1 wind chest for an organ*
> Lock Hospital Collection of Music
> *Handel's* Messiah *in score*

Magadelen Hymns [sic]
Massachusetts Compiler
1 excellent toned Spinnet

The presence of the violin and the double bass are the most expected of these items. A spinnet would refer to a small harpsichord. What is a bit more intriguing are the "elegant Barrel Organ" and the few pieces of music.

Let's briefly look at the organ before discussing the music. It would seem to be an elegant instrument, indeed, with ten barrels to it. Barrel organs (or hand organs) were mechanical instruments employed for both secular and church use. Often the cases were elegant and beautiful cabinets made by skilled craftsmen.

The oldest-surviving instrument in playing condition dates from 1502; this was no mere novelty but an instrument with a rich history. Each barrel might contain as many as eight to ten tunes.

Music for mechanical instruments such as this fell, generally, into two categories, according to Arthur W.J.G. Ord-Hume in his 1983 *Early Music* article "Ornamentation in Mechanical Music."[4] One category was music selected by the instrument builder to demonstrate its capabilities, while the other was music deliberately written for the instrument by a composer.

A barrel's arranger was often highly skilled in music himself. In the eighteenth century, G.F. Handel, C.P.E. Bach and Joseph Haydn all wrote several pieces directly for mechanical instruments. Scholars are always interested in documenting the music used in these organs; the arrangements can reveal details or clues about contemporary performance practice and which tunes were deemed popular enough to receive repeated usage.

Turning to the few pieces of written music named in McIntire's effects, we can see that he was fully aware of and apparently engaged in the musical reform movement seeded by the spiritual revival known as the First Great Awakening. He was thus a beneficiary of the "flowering of American psalmody from 1770 to 1810" due to the influence of "the singing school and the singing society rather than the church," as Nicholas Temperley in *Grove Music Online* describes it.

The metrical, unaccompanied and heterophonic "old way of singing" had been established from the earliest time in America—and in Salem—by the Ainsworth *Book of Psalmes* [sic] and the *Bay Psalm Book*. Music was sung by rote while strictly adhering to plain expression of biblical texts, which are formal in nature. A psalm was "lined out" (introduced by a leader singing one line at a time), and the congregation sang in response. Gradually, over the years, congregational use of written music was abandoned. This resulted in what many decried as offensive musical discord and textual chaos.

By 1770, William Billings (1746–1800), and the composers who followed him (now known as the First New England School), had taken up the cause of counterpoint and contrapuntal imitation, which expanded musical expression beyond the simple harmonies of preexisting hymn tunes that had been in practice since the 1720s. The singing school movement born during these years urged a return to written music or "regular singing."

The sea change represented by music such as *The Lock Hospital Chapel* collection and the Holyoke, Gram, and Holden *Massachusetts Compiler of Theoretical and Practical Elements of Sacred Vocal Music* (Boston, 1795) is an important one. It indicates a fundamental shift in thinking.

This movement urged direct and personal musical expression, with the words arising straight from singer's heart to God and sung with warmth, emotion, energy and, above all, aesthetic appeal. Yet, in post-Revolutionary America, to follow this reform movement indicates a *turning back*—an embrace of European models *over* American ones and a hunger for a more formal training in music.

> *The stately structure of this earth Jehovah did erect*
> *All the rich product of the same His curious architect*
> *—Martha Brewster, 1757*
> *—Jacob Kimball, 1800, the* Essex Harmony Tune: Plainfield

Samuel McIntire died on February 6, 1811, at age fifty-four. The *Salem Gazette* noted his demise briefly, saying the "Carver" was "very much beloved, and sincerely lamented" and would receive "a just and respectful tribute, from one who knew him well."

Published on February 12, the tribute made reference to his "uncommon native genius" and followed discussion of his architectural talents with paeans to his "admirable musical taste" and skill as "a good performer of instrumental as well as vocal music."

Added to this was testimony to McIntire's "rare endowments of the mind" and "best feelings of the heart." It should be noted that his heart had been generous enough to save a child from drowning, with subsequent damage to his health.

What makes this posthumous valentine to McIntire even more poignant, in light of his lifelong participation in Salem's musical culture, is the tiny notice to the right of this obituary:

Mr. Samuel McIntire beams at us from the only known portrait of him at the edge of the historic district that bears his name. It's not quite the same place he knew; he gazes these days at endless daily car traffic. *Courtesy of author.*

"Dancing Assembly," it announces; "the Fourth Assembly will be on TUESDAY evening next."

McIntire's rare endowments of mind and best feelings of the heart are evident also when we turn our attention to the music he left behind in his personal effects. With it, we can begin to form a deeper appreciation of the musical Mr. McIntire by analyzing the collections of music for which we have published documentation he owned.

> *The Collection of Psalm and Hymn Tunes Sung at the Chapel of the Lock Hospital. From the Last London Edition. Published in Boston in 1809. American edition of A Collection of Psalm and Hymn Tunes, Never Published Before…To Be Had at the Lock Hospital near Hyde Park Corner.* [5]

The wonderful analysis of the significance of this collection penned by scholar Nicholas Temperley in 1993 cannot be improved:

It has been generally recognized that the music of the Lock Hospital chapel was an important new influence in English and American church music during the late eighteenth and early nineteenth centuries. The chapel attracted fashionable congregations and thereby disseminated an elegant, theatrical type of hymnody that was far removed from the norms of church music… Many hymn tunes first used at the Lock Hospital became enormously popular; some still remain in common use; and their style became the model for a 'school' of hymn tunes that remained in vogue for several decades.[6]

Lock Hospital was a charity institution founded in England in 1746 for the treatment of sufferers from venereal disease. The term "lock" referred to quarantine of patients.

Charities such as the Lock Hospital, Foundling Hospital, Asylum for Female Orphans and the Magdalen Hospital developed chapels with choirs and ensembles of inmates who gave musical performances. At the Magdalen for "fallen" women, including those "seduced and abandoned," singers performed for genteel audiences—but from behind screens!

In the case of the Lock Hospital, where patients were often too ill to perform, a musically trained congregation was in order.

Musical events were calculated to attract donations and long-term patrons in addition to providing emotional sustenance for residents through the creation of music. Charity concerts became extremely popular. The Foundling Hospital endeavors, in fact, became famous for annual performances of *Messiah*, sometimes under the direction of Handel himself.

Musical selections from the Lock Hospital collection show stylistic influence from the theatrical, operatic and popular worlds; sacred sources strongly favored the Methodist–Evangelical movement sparked by brothers John and Charles Wesley.

That movement was nurtured energetically in America by the charismatic George Whitefield (1714-1770) during the spiritual revival known as the First Great Awakening, born in the early 1730s. Thundering through the land, the awakening stoked the fires for personal and emotional religious expression.

Such a movement provided a bright candle to the musical flame. The hymns of Isaac Watts's (1674–1748) songs that represented "not God's word to us, but our word to God" were of great and lasting importance in this development.

The Massachusetts Compiler of Theoretical and Practical Elements of Sacred Vocal Music: Together with a Musical Dictionary. And a Variety of Psalm tunes, Chorusses, &c. / Chiefly selected or adapted from modern European publications. Published at Boston, February, 1795, according to act of Congress.

In 1720, Rev. Thomas Symmes, of Bradford, Massachusetts, published a pamphlet called "The Reasonableness of Regular Singing, or Singing by Note." This was the sounding bell in a musical reform movement of which the first giant figure is Boston's William Billings. This movement was notable for the popularity and proliferation of the singing school and the rise of the native-born American composer. By 1801, Dr. William Bentley would refer, with chagrined exhaustion, to the accompanying flood of numberless compilations of tunes, psalms, and hymns.

Singing schools thus retrained the populace in the ability to read music. But with the coming of the Revolution, leading figures such as Billings (and others, now referred to as the First New England School) also struck a decisively rebellious and fiercely patriotic note through music. Billings's "Chester," in fact, became the de facto official Revolutionary anthem, building on the etymology of the word "chester" itself to indicate America's determination to become a fortress against tyranny.

Billings's patriotism went further. He championed, as did others, the truly indigenous American invention of advocating modification and even repudiation of accepted old European compositional techniques and elevating uniquely American modes of expression.

Billings made his views especially clear in the introduction to his 1770 *The New-England Psalm-Singer, or, American Chorister*: "I think it best for every Composer to be his own Carver…Art is subservient to genius."

The singing-school movement sparked interest in performing more challenging music. Thus we now find pieces incorporating solos, duets, and contrapuntal imitations ("fuging tunes"). Larger forms such as anthems became more popular. Choirs performed independently of the congregation.

Yet reaction to all this high-spirited "native American genius" began within a decade or two of the new nation's birth. The Revolution and its aftermath also stirred up fears and worries in some quarters of societal chaos because too many boundaries were being pushed or erased. As some became affluent, greater sophistication in all things was sought.

You can see some of this reflected in the next reforming musical impulse exemplified by the *Massachusetts Compiler* and other similar collections of music.

Boxford, Massachusetts–born composer Samuel Holyoke (1762–1820) was periodically very active in Salem. An industrious tune book compiler, in 1795 he published the *Massachusetts Compiler* in concert with composers Hans Gram (1754–1804), a Danish immigrant, and Shirley's Oliver Holden (1765–1844).

The *Massachusetts Compiler* contained not only mostly European music, in addition to some American compositions, but was prefaced by "the lengthiest exposition of music theory printed in America during the century." That alone would make it a significant force in musical practice and music publishing.

But let's focus attention on the turn back to Europe—away from the "natural genius" of Billings, a firm embrace of Old World models and standards for creating and judging excellence and taste in music.

So: was McIntire, in music if not in architecture, no longer "to be his own Carver" as Billings had urged?

This ambivalence would be of lasting influence in the American cultural scene for a century and a half to come. Remnants of it survive still in American art culture.

Samuel McIntire sleeps a hopefully peaceful sleep—well, except during October—in The Burying Point, oldest burial ground in Salem, circa 1637. *Courtesy of author.*

In the space of this section, we cannot do more than hearken to the echoes of the musical Mr. McIntire as we play through copies of his tune books on the music stand before us.

Suffice to say, Samuel McIntire, carver, may have left us much "silent music" to admire in the architecture of Salem.

But—what songs has he yet to sing to us?

PATRICK GILMORE: ROMANCING THE ANGEL

Mr. Gilmore Develops a Brain Fever

The 1869 National Peace Jubilee and Great Musical Festival To Commemorate The Restoration of Peace Throughout the Land

MR. GILMORE UNFOLDS THE PLAN TO A FRIEND, WHO DOUBTS HIS SANITY…

Her eyes were fixed upon him during the delivery of his speech with apprehensive solicitude, and at the close she exclaimed with amazement, "Why, are you crazy? Have you lost your senses?" This sudden and unexpected reply, this unappreciative reception of the first announcement of his scheme, he accepted as a declaration of war; and then and there took place the first of the series of battles that had to be fought ere the Peace Jubilee became a triumphant success.

—*P.S. Gilmore, on sharing his idea with his wife*

MORALIZING ON THE "GREAT IDEA"

Here was an enterprise to think of that should interest the whole nation, yes, the whole world, and one that had more music in it than had ever fallen upon human ear before. It was, to say the least, a very dangerous fever to have upon the brain.

—*P.S. Gilmore* [7]

What *was* that fever? Why, of course—just a monster music festival! There would be massive amounts of money to be made; massive congregations of sponsors to be enlisted; massive numbers of singers to be assembled; a huge Coliseum—with everything to be immense and the tip-top best—"colossal, stupendous, grandiose." It would be a Holy Cause, a Patriotic Duty!

How on earth could it come true?

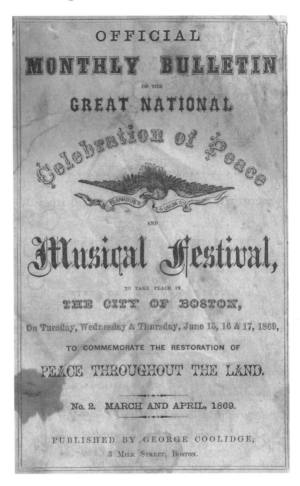

Cover of a Peace Jubilee
bulletin. *Courtesy of author.*

But it *did* come true, and P.S. Gilmore is remembered forever as its father.

*NATIONAL PEACE JUBILEE AND MUSICAL FESTIVAL,
IN BOSTON, IN HONOR OF THE RESTORATION OF THE
UNION OF THE STATES.—1869*

*Ten Thousand Singers, an Orchestra of One Thousand Instruments,
and Tens of Thousands of Spectators…Attendance of President
Grant.—Sublime and Inspiring Harmonies.—Most Majestic Musical
Demonstration of Modern Times…The Famous "Anvil" Chorus.—
Chiming the City Bells.—Novel Commingling of Artillery with Music.—
Tremendous Ovation to Grant.—Half a Million People in the City.*[8]

P.S. Gilmore's reason for mounting the grand event was clear:

In its first aspect—that of a national jubilee commemorative of the restoration of peace—it promised to strike a chord whose vibrations would reach from Maine to California. As yet no demonstration of a national character had taken place, no general rejoicing that the war was over and the Union restored, after the terrible four-years' struggle. The public mind was still disquieted by reports of lawless outbreaks in some of the States lately in rebellion...But the day of permanent peace was coming.

The *Musical Times* reported, with some dignity, on August 1, 1869:

THE BOSTON PEACE MUSICAL FESTIVAL.
TO THE EDITOR OF THE MUSICAL TIMES.
    After cavil and strife among local authorities, which at one time threatened to become serious, the Boston Peace Musical Festival has at length taken place, the use of St. James Park being granted for the erection of the Coliseum...holding between 40,000 and 50,000 persons...The Concert commenced on the 15th June...This outpouring of 10,000 voices, with organ and full orchestra, was grand in the extreme...thunders of applause breaking forth at the conclusion.

Who was this crazy, fevered fellow, P.S. Gilmore?

Flashback

Teenager Patrick S. Gilmore arrived in New York City from Ireland in October 1849. His youthful years were spent in Ballygar, although Mullingar, County Westmeath, may be his birthplace.

As with many Irish-Catholic immigrants of the era, Boston was his intended destination; he arrived in that town, joined his older brother, John Hugh Gilmore, and took a position with Boston music dealer John P. Ordway.

Although he had begun his musical endeavors in Ireland, forming a vocal quartet at his church, arranging and composing and becoming a skilled cornet player, it was in Massachusetts he was to build his amazing musical career.

The minstrel group Ordway's Aeolian Vocalists utilized his tambourine and cornet talents for a spell, but he found his true calling when he secured leadership of the Charlestown Band. He took leadership of the Suffolk Band in 1852; then the Boston Brigade Band in 1853. An invitation to lead the Salem Brass Band soon followed in 1855.

Until 1858, his talents shined in Salem. Here he polished not only the components of his own future career as an impresario, bandleader, musician, and manager but added to the luster of Salem's place in musical and cultural annals.

Under his baton, the Salem Brass Band achieved renown for musical excellence. Due to his ability to promote that band, it achieved such honors as playing for the presidential inauguration of James Buchanan in March 1857 and distinguishing the proud citizens of the City Named for Peace.

His sojourn in Salem done, he returned to Boston. His band served in the Civil War—service to which many poignant anecdotes are attached. Significantly, he organized his first large concert in New Orleans in 1864, which spearheaded the reorganization of Massachusetts military bands. Subsequent to that adventure, he resumed his Boston career as bandleader extraordinaire.

Gilmore looms large, not just by virtue of his own story, which was driven by the force of the feats he achieved and the significant force of his unique personality, but as an exemplar of nineteenth-century culture.

But—for the historian—frankly, he's a tease. A terrible flirt!

Sincerely ours: Mr. Gilmore, from the frontispiece of his own 758-page *History of the National Peace Jubilee and Great Musical Festival*. Still looking pretty darn good after his vision of the Angel. *Courtesy of author.*

Just the Facts, Ma'am?

Those who study Gilmore are hampered by several factors. Much of the available material is secondary, nonscholarly, or frankly nostalgic and hagiographic, and many oft-repeated or published stories about his life and work have compounded errors throughout the years.

In common with many other public figures, his business papers were destroyed in his lifetime and his personal property was posthumously sold, mostly for the financial support of his widow. Documentation is therefore elusive. Even examining archived notes such as those assembled locally by Frank Damon for a series of newspaper articles in 1936–37 is challenging due to Damon's omission of citation or provenance for much of his material.

Then, there is the man himself. Although he lived his life happily in the full light of public attention, his own propensities for bombastic self-promotion led him to, as one scholar felicitously puts it, give "truth a nudge in the interest of a more colorful story."

It has been speculated that Gilmore's reported early—albeit brief— association with P.T. Barnum sparked this natural tendency in him, but truth be told there were many other factors fanning that flame into life.

Now, we'll look a little more closely at Mr. Gilmore and his music, personality, and profession in the context of his times, including, of course, his time in Salem, Massachusetts.

So, pull up a haircloth-covered chair or two, Gentle Reader, and rest a bit while you still have time. It's gonna be a wild ride.

Romancing the Angel

The conception was an inspiration, which shed a lustre over one soul as bright and pure as if it were a light from heaven. When it came like a flash, filling the eye with the dazzling splendor of the scenes portrayed, and the ear with the enchanting harmony of its wonderful music, there was no thought of the scoffs, the ridicule, the derision which it would have to encounter…a struggle which threatened to strangle it at almost every step. O that it could come to pass in all the magnificence of the vision by which it was foreshadowed!
—*P.S. Gilmore*

Colossal! Stupendous! The word of the day? Expansion! Buildings were stretching upward; women's skirts were flowing outward; and the country itself was exploding westward by leaps and bounds. America dove into the romantic era—but with her own methods. Everything, it seemed, was to be "writ large," on a grand scale.

The year before nineteen-year-old Patrick Sarsfield Gilmore (1829–1892) sailed for the United States, gold was discovered in California, which sparked the monumental gold rush fever.

When he set foot on American soil in 1849, a fever for reaching far beyond earthly bounds—the movement known as Spiritualism—was also building. It would flood American culture with religious fervor; and, with increasing frequency, theatrical public display.

In 1850, singer Jenny Lind arrived in America for a two-year concert tour. Her impresario was that icon of cosmic productions, promotional genius (and cheerful humbug) P.T. Barnum. The Swedish Nightingale's concerts were often attended by near-riot conditions. Even stately Boston succumbed to the mania; one auctioned concert ticket fetched more than $600 from a fan!

So successful was Barnum's promotional machine that everywhere one turned, there was Lind, along with memorabilia, food, souvenirs, and reams of music dedicated to her with an excess of devotion—if not always with an abundance of talent. Assisting Mr. Barnum in producing some of this astonishing hoopla was recent immigrant P.S. Gilmore.

Gilmore's formative professional years encompassed the era of Harriet Beecher Stowe's *Uncle Tom's Cabin, or Life Among the Lowly*; Nathaniel Hawthorne's *The House of the Seven Gables*; Walt Whitman's *Leaves of Grass*; Herman Melville's *Moby Dick*; Henry David Thoreau's *Walden*; and Ralph Waldo Emerson's *Representative Men*.

Ideas writ large.

Orchestras came to be viewed as a huge instrument to be played by the conductor. In August 1853, French conductor Louis Antoine Jullien (1812–1860) brought orchestral Monster Concerts for the Masses to New York's Castle Garden. This "splendid, bold, and dazzlingly successful humbug," as the newspapers dubbed him, was notable for his flamboyant promotional efforts and for including the work of American musicians and composers in his concert programs. Other monster concerts of the era were mounted in South America by New Orleans–born piano virtuoso Louis Moreau Gottschalk (1829–1869).

In September 1852, as *Dwight's Journal of Music* announced, "A Grand Military Musical Festival is to come off at Castle Garden…this splendid combination of bands, never attempted before in this country…will form a great Military Orchestra of over two hundred instruments." This "first of its kind" monster band concert, according to one scholar, brought together thirteen groups, ten of which were designated as brass bands, two as cornet bands, and one lone woodwind and brass band.

John Sullivan Dwight (1813–1893), Boston's most authoritative arbiter of musical and cultural taste, subsequently groused in the April 16, 1853 edition of *Dwight's Journal of Music*, "All at once, the idea of a Brass Band shot forth: and from this prolific germ sprang up a multitude of its kind in every part of the land, like the crop of iron men from the infernal seed of the dragon's teeth. And, as if the invention of new and deadlier implements of war, which came out about the same time, had hardened mens' hearts, all the softer companions of the savage science (the woodwinds) were banished."

He reported "at least ten thousand persons, of all ages and classes, on the common" for summer concerts in the July 1853 *Journal*.

In 1855, Gilmore, fast making a name for himself as a brass band leader, was enticed from Boston to take charge of the Salem Brass Band, succeeding the group's beloved Jerome Smith, whose health was in decline. Salem's group was considered a very good local band, but Gilmore's years in Salem transformed the band's musical reputation and the man himself.

In those years, Gilmore led the band to greater public renown and enviable musical excellence. A nostalgic account, delivered in April 1900 by Thomas Carroll, speaks of Gilmore's character:

> *No one can forget the grace of Gilmore's manner…gifted in many directions, clean of heart and of speech, hating injustice and scorning meanness, with…high, poetic temperament, manly to all men and gracious towards women…a harmonious blending of courage and chivalry.*[9]

During his last year in Salem, he met and married his wife, Ellen O'Neill, from Lowell, who was an organist and choir director. He became more confident in promoting his own name and leadership as programs began to feature Gilmore's Salem Brass Band.

In 1858, he tendered his resignation, and he and his wife moved back to Boston. There he established Gilmore's Band, an independent, professional group that debuted in 1859 at Boston Music Hall.

Ten years to the day after Gilmore arrived in the United States, John Brown and a small band of fellow abolitionists invaded Harpers Ferry, Virginia (now West Virginia), hoping to spark an army of emancipation and purge slavery from the land. This accelerated the plunge toward the American Civil War.

Gilmore's band was attached to the Twenty-fourth Massachusetts Infantry Regiment and served with the Union army in a war in which carnage, too, was conducted on a grand scale.

In 1864, Gilmore organized a monster concert in Louisiana with a five-hundred-member band, six thousand singers in the chorus, fifty cannons, and forty anvil-striking soldiers. All this was for the inauguration of the new governor, Michael Hahn. This typically heroic feat sealed Gilmore's fame.

Twenty years after Gilmore landed on U.S. shores, he produced the National Peace Jubilee and Great Musical Festival. Organized with a volatile combination of the purest Romantic idealism and dogged practical persistence, Gilmore's festival would require him to build, in H. Wiley Hitchcock's succinct description,

> *a three-and-a-half acre Coliseum...*[he] *issued periodic rehearsal orders like a battlefield general to 100 choral organizations totaling 10,296 singers;* [he] *inveigled the great Ole Bull into being concertmaster of 525*

Old Town Hall's Market Square.
From C.H. Webber and Winfield S. Nevins's Old Naumkeag: An Historical Sketch of the City of Salem, and the Towns of Marblehead, Peabody, Beverly, Danvers, Wenham, Manchester, Topsfield, and Middleton.

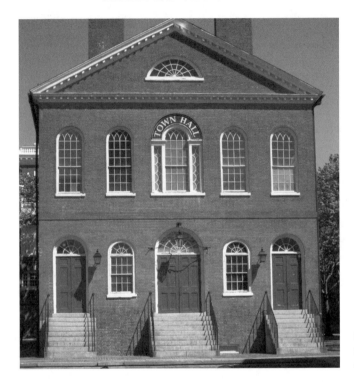

Old Town Hall today. *Courtesy of author.*

orchestra players; commandeered a band of 486 wind and percussion players…It lasted five days…its climax was the "Anvil Chorus" from Verdi's Il Trovotore *for the entire massed ensemble plus electrically operated city bells and a dozen cannon.*[10]

It was a great success.

And—better still—the first Jubilee even made money! (Alas…'twas not to be the case with the second one.)

The story of the Jubilee is recounted in exhaustive detail by Gilmore in his Romantic manifesto par excellence, the massive *History of the National Peace Jubilee and Great Musical Festival,* published in 1871. This amazing tome of more than 750 pages brims with passion, pathos, humor, and sly wit.

In the language of religious devotion to the service of music and the Angel of Peace, our hero takes us from the moment of his divine inspiration through his obsession in pursuing his vision, the ordeal of raising money, and grinding of teeth and shouts of joy—and literal angelic visions.

By the time the final triumphant chapter arrives, Gentle Reader, you might feel you, too, have fired the cannon, rung the bells, and sung with the vast chorus the words of Oliver Wendell Holmes (to the tune of Matthias Keller's *American Hymn*) "Angel of Peace, thou hast wandered too long!"

But oh, what awesome musical treasures that Angel, Gilmore's envisioned life partner, brought to Salem, a city named for peace; to Boston, home to the second-oldest peace society in the United States; and thus, ultimately, to humankind.

"AT THE SOURCE OF THE LONGEST RIVER" —T.S. ELIOT'S SALEM ROOTS

Author's note: Archaic spellings can be confusing for modern readers, especially since sometimes the spelling of a name or place changes when written at different times, or even within the same document! Therefore, Eliot's ancestors' names have been standardized in this section, except when used in direct quotes.

Beginnings–Andrew Eliott

Old men ought to be explorers
Here and there does not matter
We must be still and still moving
Into another intensity
For a further union, a deeper communion
Through the dark cold and the empty desolation,
The wave cry, the wind cry, the vast waters
Of the petrel and the porpoise.
In my end is my beginning.
—T.S. Eliot, "East Coker" (number two of Four Quartets*)*

A plain and modest memorial plaque for Thomas Stearns Eliot hangs on the wall in a quiet little corner of St. Michael's Church in the rustic village of East Coker, Somerset, England. "Of your charity," it reads, "pray for the repose of the soul of Thomas Stearns Eliot, Poet, 26th September 1888–4th January 1965." Arching over and above this plea on the earth-hued oval are inscribed quotes from the first and last lines of Eliot's poem *East Coker*: "In my beginning is my end" and "In my end is my beginning."[11]

Sometime after 1668, Andrew Eliott emigrated from East Coker, Somersetshire, England, where he had been baptized in 1627, according to the research of William Richard Cutter, which was published in 1908.

The Elliott family had deep roots in Somerset (England), with Norman origins and Scottish branches. Andrew Eliott came first to Salem by sea, and settled shortly thereafter in Beverly, which became, in 1683, a lawful port of entry and was annexed to Salem. Eliott was evidently well thought of because he was quickly entrusted with important duties in Beverly.

> *the 2: day of nouember 1686 Att a Generall Town meeting Legally warned there were Chosen Select men for the year ensuing: viz*
> *Capt. Thorndike   Leut John Dodg*
> *Sargent John Hill   Sargent Peter woodberrie*
> *Lift Andrew Elliott*

As one of his duties, Andrew was also entrusted with the money to pay a "Mr. Baker of Boston" for "our bell hanging in Beverly meeting house." Also, "Eight shillings to be Laid out to buy Clothing for Illegitimate Daughter of Benjamin Trask…The aboumentioned: 8s: that was by the aboue order to be Liad out for clothing for the abouesd Childe was Laid out to best aduantage for said Childe and sd Clothing Deliuered vnto the wife of Joseph Hibbert for sd Childes vse." [*sic*] He was also chosen to serve as commissioner in 1688.[12]

In 1686 "Andrew Elliott, SENR," was called upon to witness the execution of an important legal document.

> *All ye said Township of Salem, viz: all that tract and parcell of land, lying to ye westward of Neumkeage River, alias Bassriver, whereupon ye Town of Salem is built, so proceeding along to ye head of Neumkeage River, called by ye English, Bassriver, so comprehending all ye land belonging to the Township of Salem according as it is butted and bounded with and upon ye towns of Beverly, Wenham, Topsfield, Redding, Linne and Marblehead, down to ye sea—which said land is a part of what belonged to the ancestors of ye granters…to be hereby granted & sold unto ye…for ye sole use, benefitt and behoof of ye Proprietors in & Purchasers of ye said Township of Salem… In witness—whereof…the eleventh day of October Anno Domini One Thousand Six Hundred Eighty & Six—Annog Regni Regis Jacob II di Anglia, Scotia, Francia & Irylernia, Fidei Defensoris Secundo.*[sic][13]

Elliott's signature appears first in a list of five witnesses to this deed, executed between Native Americans and settlers, to purchase the land from its original owners for twenty pounds, upon which the township of Salem would flourish.

Elliott was an educated man and wrote well. He thus left some glimpses of his character. In a heartbreakingly poignant note, he recorded the death of his son, Andrew Jr:

> *the dear and only son of Andrew Elliott whose mother's name was [Grace] and was born in East Coker in the county of Somerset in Old England being on board of vessel appertaining unto Philip English of Salem, one Bavidge being master…was violently thrown into the sea and there perished in the water, to the great grief of his said father the penman hereof, being aged about 37 years on the 12th day of September about 10 of the clock in the morning…in the year of our Lord God 1688. Deep meditation surely every man in his best estate is wholly vanitie.*[14]

The father's cry from a broken heart, a "deep meditation" indeed upon human loss and its meaning, resonates down through the centuries.

> *The only wisdom we can hope to acquire*
> *Is the wisdom of humility: humility is endless.*
> *The houses are all gone under the sea.*
> *The dancers are all gone under the hill.*
> *T.S. Eliot, "East Coker"*

The First Church of Beverly admitted "Mr. Andrew Eliot" to "full communion" on February 24, 1687, according to an entry in an Essex Institute Historical Collection reprint of a chronicle on the early records of the church. According to the same source, his wife was admitted in 1681.

On April 11, 1690, Elliott, at the age of sixty-three, became the first elected town clerk of Beverly. Beverly's records, previously entrusted to the hands of various selectmen, had been kept since 1665, and Eliott had been transcribing town records into an improved book format prior to obtaining his official—and compensated—post.

According to a town history published in 1843, Eliott's notation in the town's second volume of records in November 1685 referred readers to a "parchment-covered old book extant" for "former concerns in this matter."

> *At a "ffree mens meeting holden on Wednesday ye 27th Day of Aprill 1692: Andrew Elliott was Chosen & appointed by sd ffreemen to serue as*

a representatiue for our Town of Beuerly for ye first sessions of ye Generall Court holden at Boston on ye 4th Day of may 1692. [sic] "

He served for several years as a representative to the general court.

In 1692, Elliott was given another important role in regional history: that of a juror in the Salem witch trials. By serving in this capacity, he helped send innocent people to their ignominious and untimely deaths.

One wonders what he thought about seeing the English family name appear on the roll call of the accused witches.

It is known how he felt about his service in the aftermath, however. After the witchcraft hysteria died down, he and his fellow jurors made a public recantation of the condemnations and executions they had facilitated and, in that document, confessed:

> *We were sadly deluded and mistaken—for which we are much disquieted and distressed in our minds, and do therefore humbly beg forgiveness, first of God, for Christ's sake, for this our error…and we also pray that we may be considered candidly and aright by the living sufferers, as being then under the power of a strong and general delusion.* [15]

Of these bits and pieces the interior life of a human being can sometimes glimpsed, but documentation falls silent and time draws the curtain once more.

Andrew Elliott—immigrant from East Coker and progenitor of the American branch of the Eliot family, from which Thomas Stearns Eliot would bloom—died March 1, 1703-1704, at the age of seventy-six. His will mentioned his second wife of more than four decades, Mary; several children, including those deceased; and grandchildren.

In the stillness of the tiny village of East Coker, rural and green, the whisper of a poetic running stream found its source. Soon it would flow, riverlike, to the sea and shores of New England.

For the American-born and England-loving T.S. Eliot, the music of that river, fed and freshened over the centuries, would eventually return him to England, leaving his ashes to the care of an ancient home and the dawn wind. That whispered stream became the music of a life hungering to live at life's very source.

> *On a Summer midnight, you can hear the music*
> *…Mirth of those long since under earth*
> *Nourishing the corn. Keeping time,*

Naumkeag Notations

An Archway at Beauport–
Sleeper-McCann House at
Eastern Point, Gloucester
Courtesy of author.

Keeping the rhythm in their dancing
As in their living in the living seasons
…Out at sea the dawn wind
Wrinkles and slides. I am here
Or there, or elsewhere. In my beginning.
—*T.S. Eliot, "East Coker"*

Beginnings—Isaac Stearns

The river is within us, the sea is all about us;
The sea is the land's edge also, the granite
Into which it reaches, the beaches where it tosses
Its hints of earlier and other creation
…The sea has many voices,
Many gods and many voices.
The salt is on the briar rose,
The fog is in the fir trees.
—*T.S. Eliot, "The Dry Salvages"* (number three of Four Quartets)

In March, 1630, Puritan leader Hon. John Winthrop, Esq., sailed from England, bound for the New World, "with a great company of Religious people, of which Christian tribes he was the Brave Leader and famous Governor." On board his flagship, *Arbella*, he began a journal of their New-England enterprise that commenced, appropriately enough, on Easter Monday, March 29. Rocked by the waves on their English ark, Winthrop also penned a detailed description of the spiritual and worldly course he and his community were to follow.

He wrote:

> *We are entered into Covenant with Him for this worke. Wee haue taken out a commission...Wee have hereupon besought Him of favour and blessing. Now if the Lord shall please to heare us, and bring us in peace to the place we desire, then hath hee ratified this covenant and sealed our Commission, and will expect a strict performance of the articles contained in it.* [sic][16]

The *Arbella* came to the shores of Massachusetts and landed at Salem in June 1630, and its passengers disembarked to begin their great mission. This mission was to establish, quite consciously, before the "eyes of all people," a pioneering plantation of faith and fellowship, that oft-proclaimed model of a purified, divinely centered and sanctified "city upon a hill."

Aboard the *Arbella* with Winthrop and his company, according to the scholarship of Henry Bond and others, was Isack Sternes [*sic*], most probably emigrating from the Parish of Nayland in Suffolk, England.[17]

Soon after the arrival of the other ships in Winthrop's fleet, Winthrop moved the center of operations to the mouth of the Charles River, and Stearns settled at Watertown, near Mount Auburn. He bears the distinction of being admitted a freeman May 18, 1631, which was, it is noted, the "earliest date of any such admission." Serving for several years as a selectman, Stearns was also involved in the planning of the first bridge over the Charles River at Watertown.

Stearns was affluent and owned a substantial homestead that included meadowlands, marshes, uplands, fourteen lots and 467 acres by the time of his death in June 1671, forty-one years almost to the day after he landed at Salem.

He left behind his beloved wife, Mary, and seven children, all of whom received generous bequests. His was a life lived in fulfillment of covenants, and he could point with pride to the evidence of his heavenly father's "favour and blessing."

"I return my spirit into the hands of God that gave it," he proclaimed in his last testament, "and my body to the earth, from whence it was taken."[18]

Eventually, of this line, would issue Charlotte Champe Stearns, who, with Henry Ware Eliot—far removed from New England's stony harbors and wave-tossed beaches—would produce another seven children. Thomas Stearns, born September 26, 1888, grew up in the frontier town of St. Louis, Missouri, on the banks of the Mississippi, but he was nevertheless surrounded by an ever-present consciousness of his New England, Puritan and moralistic ancestry, fortified and memorialized by both parents—especially his mother.

From both the Eliot and Stearns sides of Tom's family, he inherited a predisposition to the fervor of spiritual enterprise. An uncle, Rev. Oliver Stearns, held forth at Harvard Divinity School, and both his maternal and paternal lines had produced several other preachers and theologians.

The most decisive childhood influences on the young writer's sense of stern ancestral mission stemmed from the example of his grandfather, Rev. William Greenleaf Eliot, the "Saint of the West." Traveling to the frontier

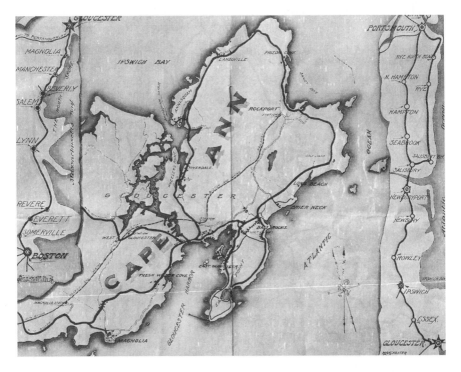

Map from pamphlet "The Charm of Old Cape Ann in Massachusetts" from the Chamber of Commerce, Gloucester, Massachusetts. *Courtesy the collection of the Institute for Music, History, and Cultural Traditions.*

after leaving Harvard Divinity School, Rev. Eliot would found the Unitarian Church in St. Louis in the 1830s.

This august forefather also founded Washington University and Smith Academy, a preparatory school. Tom's mother wrote a biography of her father-in-law to firmly fix the example of the revered man in her children's minds and hearts. Although Rev. Eliot died the year before Tom was born, he was ever present in the Eliot household.

And Charlotte Eliot, herself, wrote religious poetry that extolled the ecstatic joys of spiritual pilgrimage and uncompromising moral leadership.

Tom Eliot spent the first sixteen years of his life in the urban setting of the burgeoning, raw and pulsating city of St. Louis. Moreover, he lived in a family house which, over the years, occupied an oasis in an increasingly declining neighborhood.

A Boston North Shore Childhood

However, each summer, for the first eight years of his life, the family would travel back to New England, staying at the Hawthorne Inn at Gloucester, Cape Ann. In 1896, his father built a house on Gloucester's Eastern Point.

There Tom grew to young adulthood and reveled each summer in the sights and sounds of the sea on a spot "surrounded by wild bush" and looking out on a harbor dotted by white sails, its waves edged by granite. He delighted in the birds and the beaches and loved sailing; all were sustaining joys in his life.

He became intimately familiar with the rocky coast of the North Shore, including the formations called the Dry Salvages that lie northeast of Rockport. There are those in Gloucester who recall him. "As a young man, T.S. Eliot would wander Main Street in Gloucester, penetrating every shop window that he passed by."[19]

Thus Eliot's formative years encompassed both the sense and sights of urban decay—the many moods of the flowing Mississippi River—and the open, haunting call of the sea on the North Shore of Massachusetts, especially at Cape Ann (which is also a location of significance in Salem's early history).

Though he would cross that sea to go back to his deepest ancestral roots and eventually become England's own great poet, Eliot would come to acknowledge his American roots in interviews. To the discerning reader, those legacies also permeate his work.

Naumkeag Notations

I do not know much about gods; but I think that the river
Is a strong brown god—sullen, untamed and intractable
…Keeping his seasons and rages, destroyer, reminder
Of what men choose to forget.
—*T.S. Eliot, "The Dry Salvages"*

In a 1959 issue of the *Paris Review*, Eliot was interviewed by Donald Hall, who asked, "Do you think there's a connection with the American past?"

Eliot, who throughout his life had striven to be "more English than the English," answered, "Yes, but I couldn't put it any more definitely than that, you see…putting it as modestly as I can, it wouldn't be what it is if I'd been born in England, and it wouldn't be what it is if I'd stayed in America. It's a combination of things. But in its sources, in its emotional springs, it comes from America." [20]

Let's take a look at T.S. Eliot's own life and work to help illuminate the gifts and challenges alike of his spiritual and professional inheritance from those English men and women who stepped ashore at Salem and to explore the resonance that inheritance provides for us.

The moment of the rose and the moment of the yew-tree
Are of equal duration. A people without history
Is not redeemed from time, for history is a pattern
Of timeless moments.
—*T.S. Eliot, "Little Gidding" (number four of Four Quartets)*

It is worth noting that Eliot's Stearns forefather on the *Arbella* was Major William Hathorne, Nathaniel Hawthorne's paternal ancestor. Hawthorne's lineage also, of course, included Justice John Hathorne, fearsome magistrate at the Salem witch trials.

T.S. Eliot was distantly related to Nathaniel Hawthorne, according to biographer Lyndall Gordon, "on the Hathorn[*sic*] side."

T.S. Eliot, who achieved the lofty status of Nobel Prize winner and, significantly, became one of his generation's most authoritative cultural critics, ironically remarked on his genetic inheritance from witch-hangers and the cultural debt he owed to his common heritage with Nathaniel Hawthorne.

Indeed, as even a superficial acquaintance with American literature will reveal, Eliot's sensibilities and literary soul had much in common with Hawthorne's work and with that other eminent American expatriate, Henry James.

In a 1972 *New England Quarterly* article by John J. Soldo, reference is made to yet another Eliot ancestor, William Dawes, Paul Revere's oft-overlooked colleague in patriotic alarm raising, and to Eliot's familial connections to political luminaries, such as the Adamses, and to Rutherford B. Hayes.[21]

Eliot was also related to Charles W. Eliot, longtime president of Harvard, where young Tom was educated as his grandfather had been.

His formidable grandfather, the missionary Rev. William Greenleaf Eliot Jr., who advocated for women's rights and prohibition—and who was, in Gordon's description, the "only open abolitionist" in antebellum St. Louis—looms large in the genetic and psychological influences of T.S. Eliot.

And, as Soldo points out, one must add to this a serious strain of repressed elitism that Eliot also inherited—nay, was taught to embody—as scion of a family with deep New England roots.

Eastern Point in Gloucester *Courtesy of author.*

Yet, for all this we must give significant weight to the impact of Eliot's own unique childhood and formative experiences. His childhood was split between St. Louis, Missouri, a pioneering, frontierlike and evolving culture, and his yearly rhythmic return to the deeper-rooted, yet—and this is truly key—also *evolving* New England culture of the North Shore and Boston.

This, along with his "strong sense of mission," which was so often referred to in any number of sources and so clearly evident in his body of work, are some of the most important keys to understanding his development as an artist and, indeed, as a man.

This American expatriate, who became a British citizen after converting to High Anglicism (Anglo-Catholicism) in 1927, nevertheless expressed in significant ways his complex understanding of his New England ancestral heritage.

Note the crosscurrents evident in this passage: "Those of us who can claim any New England ancestors may congratulate ourselves that we are their descendants, and at the same time rejoice that we are not their contemporaries."

He continued:

> *They were the men who carried American commerce to the Levant, to India, to China…They built the fine old ships which we know only from contemporaneous engravings…for them was built the handsome old custom house at Salem, now slumbering in proud uselessness. Go to Salem and see a town that flourished a hundred years ago in the high tide of New England's naval energy. It seems now to be always in dignified mourning for its former grandeur, for the ships which do not leave and the ships which do not return.* [22]

Eliot's work cannot be understood without also understanding him as a sailor "in the stillness / Between two waves of the sea."

> *We shall not cease from exploration*
> *And the end of all our exploring*
> *Will be to arrive where we started*
> *And know the place for the first time.*
> *Through the unknown, remembered gate*
> *When the last of earth left to discover*
> *Is that which was the beginning;*
> *At the source of the longest river.*
> —*T.S. Eliot, "Little Gidding"*

Meeting Mr. Eliot

The study of T.S. Eliot's work has generated an endless sea of critical assessments, appreciations, and the like, so much so that the researcher can easily feel like building a replica of the *Arbella* herself with which to navigate the currents. (Or perhaps, just crashing the boat onto the Dry Salvages near Gloucester—taking along, of course, a volume of Eliot's poems for consolation amid the wreckage.)

Yet because of Eliot's own stricture against facilitating biographical study of his life, and thanks to second wife and widow Valerie Eliot's unceasing role as guardian of his work and reputation, biographies are few.

Available biographies include the first, *T.S. Eliot: A Life* by Peter Ackroyd, published in 1984, and Lyndall Gordon's *T.S. Eliot: An Imperfect Life*, a well-researched (if sometimes overly inferential) tome, published in 1998.

More recently, a slightly overheated biography of Eliot's first wife, called *Painted Shadow: A Life of Vivienne Eliot* (2001), by Carole Seymour-Jones, has voyaged out. It offers a rather interesting view of Eliot and one that, with the anticipated opening of his papers, should make for another deluge of scholarly ink.

Even quoting from his poetry, until recently, was difficult—if not impossible. Luckily, these strictures are easing. According to publications such as London's the *Evening Standard*, there are already three major new works being planned.[23]

Like any other artist, Eliot's work evolved in style, content, aesthetic sense, and purpose. All artists are products of their times and their artistic and human inheritances as well as exemplars of their own individual muse. No human being nor human endeavor can be understood without understanding them in *context*, especially in historical context.

Discussing Eliot's work has long been complicated by the attention paid to his own pronouncements on the nature of his work—the mission of poetry and the poet. Adding to that is the power of his still-influential voice as a cultural and literary critic.

This phenomenon is, in itself, worthy of reexamination, and some of the recent literature on Eliot is beginning to do just that.

For the purposes of our current discussion, we'll remain perched at the edge of this metaphorical ocean. Listening to the cadence and music of his poetry as our touchstone and guide, we can truly go to the source of that long, long river.

Here on the North Shore, however, one can also indulge in physical proximity to the actual ocean, which is so important to Eliots of both distant and recent pasts. There, seaside and listening, we can contemplate the forces that both divided and united all the elements of the genius of T.S. Eliot.

> *But heard, half-heard, in the stillness*
> *Between two waves of the sea.*
> *Quick now, here, now, always—*
> *A condition of complete simplicity*
> *(Costing not less than everything)*
> *And all shall be well and*
> *All manner of thing shall be well*
> *When the tongues of flame are in-folded*
> *Into the crowned knot of fire*
> *And the fire and the rose are one.*
> —*T.S. Eliot, "Little Gidding"*

A LIFE LIVED IN HARMONY:
COMPOSER ARTHUR FOOTE

They were twenty-five miles away, but they could see the flames of the Salem disaster from their New Hampshire summer home, Rest Harrow, which was not far from Amesbury, Massachusetts. The terrible Salem Fire of 1914 left thousands homeless and devastated the city's landscape. A victim of the conflagration was a small house at 44 Warren Street—composer Arthur Foote's childhood home, where he was born on March 5, 1853.

Arthur Foote's name may not readily come to your mind when thinking of important American composers; yet, historian Nicholas Tawa describes him as "one of the most important American composers in the last quarter of the nineteenth century and first two decades of the twentieth century…the musical world of Foote's day highly respected him as an educator, keyboard performer, and choral music director, and could not praise his music highly enough." [24]

Indeed, he was so esteemed in his lifetime that on Thanksgiving Day in 1914, when it became known he had suffered a serious illness, organists throughout the entire country "by concerted arrangement, played his Festival March in F as an expression of gratitude for his recovery."

Foote's family had deep roots in America; antecedents arrived on these shores from England circa 1635 and eventually settled in Salem. Several Footes went to sea, and his great-grandfather served under Washington during the 1775 siege of Boston.

His parents' marriage was a happy one, and it is charming to note that they met through a mutual love of and involvement in singing and music.

Arthur's father, Caleb, born in 1803, was the son of a sea captain and was orphaned young. He became an apprentice in 1817 at the biweekly *Salem Gazette* and, by 1833, through hard work and self-improvement he was not only editor but sole owner of the newspaper. He continued at the *Gazette* until 1888. He also served on the Salem School Committee, at the state level as a representative; and was appointed Salem postmaster in 1841. He died in 1894.

His mother, Mary Wilder (White) Foote, rejoiced in Arthur's birth when she was forty-three since the Footes had sadly lost several children before him.

Mary was born in 1810, in Newburyport, Massachusetts. The family moved to Salem after her mother's death a few months later. She first mentions meeting Caleb Foote in a November 1831 journal entry, where she relates she spent the evening singing with "Mr. and Mrs. Upham, David Mack, and Mr. Foote." Mary sang in the choir of First Church and was reported to have a "voice of great range and sweetness." After her marriage, she also edited a book column for the *Gazette*.[25]

The Peabodys and Emersons were friends, and they were particularly happy when Sophia Peabody married Nathaniel Hawthorne, being fans of his work. Letters between Sophia and Mary shared tidings of their respective family lives, especially the happy events.

Arthur's mother Mary died in 1857. Thus, he was raised by his father—who remained unmarried for the next forty years—and his older sister Mary (1843–1934). He also had an older brother, Henry Wilder (1838–1889). The siblings remained very close and quite supportive of each other throughout their lives.

The future successful composer, performer, educator, and musical entrepreneur grew up "within a stone's throw or at least a golf drive of Gallows Hill" and, later in life, wrote a fond accounting of his upbringing in Salem.

In his autobiography,[26] Foote described the Salem of his youth. "Salem in those days was a delightful place to live in. There was contentment and good average prosperity; with small incomes there was still ease."

He described the beauty of Salem with a true lover's voice, particularly its many gardens—"an enormous bed of tulips in the Cabot garden, for the flowering of which we watched every year…the gardens of Salem were unusual in their excellence and variety." His father, Caleb, gave Arthur three

Gravestone of Caleb
Foote at Salem's Harmony
Grove Cemetery. *Courtesy
of author.*

pear trees of his very own, and the land around 44 Warren Street blossomed
with a large garden, fruit trees, and berry bushes.

Foote's Salem was "a city of about 20,000…well governed and its
affairs well managed…We had one series of first-rate lectures and another
consisting partly of lectures and partly of good concerts. We had a life of our
own, and were not dependent upon Boston."

Among his many boyhood activities, he recounted attending a dancing
class at Hamilton Hall, where "the famous Papanti was the teacher,"
and sailing, rowing, playing baseball and enjoying the trapeze at a town
gymnasium. During that time, there were cows that regularly made early
morning and evening trips along Essex or Warren Streets; fire engines were
pumped by hand; the Eastern Railroad took forty-five minutes to reach
Boston; and Foote and his friends regularly treated themselves to "three-cent
turnovers, mince and apple, and Salem 'Gibraltars' and 'Black Jacks.'"

Arthur, who ostensibly seemed destined for a career in law or as his
father's successor as editor at the *Salem Gazette*, discovered music as a boy; in

1865, he began piano lessons with Fanny Paine (his sister studied with Salem musical luminary Manuel Fenollosa). His family was supportive of his desire to pursue music, much to their credit.

During his formative years, Foote reports, he read the extremely influential *Dwight's Journal of Music*, which, in exchange for copies of the *Gazette*, came as a complimentary offering to the newspaper office. The *Journal* stressed a conservative Germanic tradition (e.g. Bach, Beethoven and Handel) without enthusiasm for more contemporary music (e.g. Wagner, Liszt, or even Brahms).

Foote's Salem years enriched him by association with two well-respected local musicians. The first, physician John Francis Tuckerman, advocated "the cultivation of a purer and higher style of music." Tuckerman led the choirs of North Church and, later, Grace Church, which was built during Arthur's youth.

"General" Henry Kemble Oliver (1800–1885) was even more influential in Salem, and his musical accomplishments were many: Salem Glee Club, Salem's Mozart Society, organist at three churches and president of the Salem Oratorio Society. Oliver, born in Beverly and educated at Harvard and Dartmouth, was mayor of Lawrence and later of Salem; he also served as treasurer of Massachusetts and headed the state Department of Labor.

It is quite commonly known that Oliver composed the hymn tune *Federal Street*, but his output included *Beacon Street*, *Grove*, *Harmony* and *Morning*; he also compiled several hymn tune collections, including one with Dr. Tuckerman.

With these early influences to sustain him and with his family's unwavering support both emotionally and financially, Arthur moved into serious study of music in Boston and entered Harvard in 1870.

It was a fortuitous time to enter Harvard; the school was—under the guidance of President Dr. Charles W. Eliot (1834–1926)—expanding into a real university. One of the most important outcomes of this development is that Arthur Foote, while studying under composer John Knowles Paine (1839–1906), became the first American composer to receive a master's degree in music; his 1875 thesis was called "The Development of the Secular Style in Music." Foote's first published piece of music was his *Class Song, 1874*, which was written for the commencement of his graduating class.

Arthur Foote's subsequent career became a model of a successful working musician, after a slow and ultimately unsuccessful start in Salem as a music instructor. Although he would return to Salem for brief periods, 1876 saw him living in Boston.

Then, as now, the culture of the United States provided artists with many challenges in pursuing their vocations. Thus Foote's main task at the beginning of his career was to establish himself in the rapidly expanding metro-Boston area. He began to craft a living by teaching, performing as a church organist, and as a musical entrepreneur.

The Greater Boston area nurtured well-educated professional and knowledgeable core audiences that appreciated the importance of the arts, education, and literature to the vitality of the city and its growth.

The general audience for cultivated and art music had been further augmented by the success of massive Peace Jubilees, in which thousands of Americans participated as performers and audience members. Both extravaganzas were held in Boston and organized by bandleader Patrick Gilmore. One residual effect of these events, Foote noted, was to spark a more widespread interest in music among the ordinary citizens of the region.

In addition, the latter part of the nineteenth century and the first decades of the twentieth saw the establishment of important organizations: the

Arthur Foote, circa 1920.
From Grove's Dictionary of Music and Musicians—American Supplement.

Boston Conservatory, founded in 1867 by Julius Eichberg; the New England Conservatory, also founded in 1867, by Eben Tourjée; and the Boston Symphony Orchestra, which was started in 1881 by Henry Higginson.

Foote writes in his 1937 *Musical Quarterly* article, "A Bostonian Remembers," that:

> *Boston's musical renown very soon came to be not only national but international. The programs of the Boston Symphony Orchestra showed from the first a rightly hospitable attitude towards American compositions and have continued to do so.*[27]

Foote's career extended over fifty years. In addition to being the first native-born and native-trained American composer to win international renown—a remarkable achievement for his era when American music was waging an uphill battle for respect in comparison to European music—

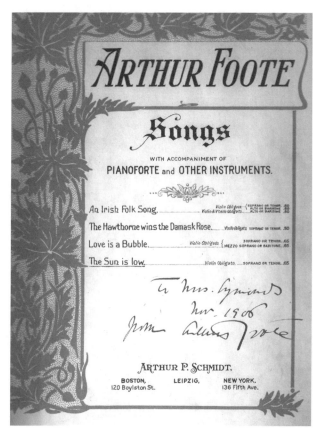

Cover of sheet music with autograph of the composer. *Courtesy of author.*

his work in the fields of theory and education and his untiring devotion to establishing and nurturing a thriving professional concert culture left a luminous legacy.

He produced chamber works, orchestral works, works for organ and piano, and a great number of sacred and secular songs that were performed by a variety of artists; for instance, singer John McCormack particularly enjoyed singing *The Song by the Mill*. His *Irish Folk Song* and *I'm Wearin' Awa, Jean* were considered particularly charming pieces, to which this singer can attest, having performed them with great appreciation for Foote's harmonic subtlety and respect for the cadence of language.

Foote died after a four-day bout with pneumonia on April 8, 1937. In his last hours, according to his nephew, he "lay quietly, eyes closed, his fingers moving across the coverings as though he were playing the piano, or his hand beating time…as tho [*sic*] listening to an orchestra…I don't think I've known another man so widely and deeply loved, as well as honored for his gifts and graces. And he was the soul of integrity and honor."[28]

Arthur Foote was buried in Mount Auburn Cemetery. His wife, Kate, died April 8, 1943; his daughter, Katherine, also a musician and singer, died in Maine in 1970. She and her husband had no children.

Thus Salem's Arthur Foote must live on for us only through his music—a worthy legacy, all in all.

SUMMER STORMS, STORY NOVELISTS: HAWTHORNE AND MELVILLE

"All I can say is that I religiously seclude myself, every morning…and remain in retirement till dinner-time…But the summer is not my natural season for work; and I often find myself gazing at Monument Mountain, broad before my eyes, instead of at the infernal sheet of paper under my hand," Nathaniel Hawthorne wrote his publisher, James Fields, from La Rouge Maison, the little red Lenox farmhouse in which he and his family had lived since the spring of 1850.

The Hawthornes rented the house for $150 a year from the Tappan family. He had arrived in the Berkshires "harassed in spirit" as a refugee from an unfortunate turn of events in Salem.

There, in his hometown, an intense political scandal had erupted with Hawthorne at the center. The fracas cost him his position at the Custom House.

Hawthorne stamps from the first day of issue. *Courtesy of author.*

Sketch of the Hawthorne home, circa 1877. *From C.H. Webber and Winfield S. Nevins's* Old Naumkeag: An Historical Sketch of the City of Salem, and the Towns of Marblehead, Peabody, Beverly, Danvers, Wenham, Manchester, Topsfield, and Middleton.

Hardly is he an innocent caught in the storm. Hawthorne himself had contributed to the volatility of the situation.

In a contemporary letter to Henry Wadsworth Longfellow, he wrote, "I must confess it stirs up a little of the devil within me to find myself hunted by these political bloodhounds…I may perhaps select a victim, and let fall a little drop of venom in his heart, that shall make him writhe before the grin of the multitude for a considerable time to come." [29]

Yet after this much-bruited "public decapitation"—suitably rendered after he boiled awhile in a seething cauldron of political porridge—the effect has been positive: his literary spirit was set free.

Energized and bolstered by his understanding and encouraging wife Sophia, he had exchanged a materially safe if stolid existence for a freer, yet uncertain, one of imagination and literary success. His prospects for that success are solid, however, since Hawthorne's literary reputation had finally taken firm hold with the success of his novel *The Scarlet Letter.*

Written with a pen dipped in the gloom of his political donnybrook and in the shadow of his mother's death, this novel had set him on his true path.

He bloomed with the encouragement of a supportive and appreciative publisher and turned out his most successful work.

In Lenox, he hammered away at writing *The House of the Seven Gables,* while he wiped his pen on the red lining of the royal purple writing gown fashioned by his wife. (Sophia would eventually sew an appliqué, shaped like a butterfly, on that spot—to defend the cloth.)

Outside, Hawthorne's children spilled from this "smallest of ten-feet houses," as they laughed and played on the idyllically beautiful Stockbridge Bowl lakeshore and in the thick woods of Highwood, which was immortalized as Tanglewood in Hawthorne's books for children.

Yet, paradise is finite.

"I find I do not feel at home among these hills…I do not get acclimated to the peculiar state of the atmosphere…and am none so vigorous as I used to be on the seacoast." On a sleety winter day, the family finally left the Berkshires.

Left behind were the household cats and friend and neighbor Herman Melville.

Melville's masterpiece, *Moby Dick,* which was dedicated to Hawthorne in "admiration for his genius," was newly published at the time. Melville's own literary talents were in sudden and lush bloom.

Melville had pursued his friendship with Hawthorne, which inspired him to do the greatest work of his life, as single-mindedly as Ahab followed the fin. The departure of his idol threw him into deep depression. He struggled in his intense work.

Melville and Hawthorne met on a mountain climb in a fierce summer storm, which erupted during a mountainside party at the culmination

The Custom House at Salem Maritime National Historic Site, where Nathaniel Hawthorne had his office until he was—umm—downsized. *Courtesy of author.*

Inside Arrowhead, Herman Melville's home in Pittsfield, Massachusetts. A registered National Historic Landmark, it is also the site of the Berkshire Historical Society. Herman would be *so* proud. *Courtesy of author.*

of the trek. The rocky walls rang with poetry—William Cullen Bryant's "Monument Mountain" declaimed to its very last syllable—and heads bubbled with champagne.

Their meeting has been described often. However, the *parting* of these two literary figures closed one chapter and yet ignites curiosity in one of the most oddly intriguing relationships in American literary history—a relationship that was fraught with undercurrents and overlaid with obfuscation for years to come.

Melville wrote to Hawthorne in November 1851, saying:

> *Appreciation! Recognition! Is love appreciated?...your appreciation is my glorious gratuity...A sense of unspeakable security is in me this moment, on account of your having understood the book. I have written a wicked*

Statue of Nathaniel Hawthorne in Salem, Massachusetts He isn't perched on the steps of the Custom House, for which he is probably quite grateful. *Courtesy of author.*

Custom House in Derby Square. Salem's historic global importance in overseas trade is marked by the fact that there have been cuftom houses in Salem since 1649. *Courtesy of author.*

book, and feel spotless as the lamb…Whence come you, Hawthorne? By what right do you drink from my flagon of life? And when I put it to my lips—lo, they are yours and not mine. I feel that the Godhead is broken up like the bread at the Supper, and that we are the pieces. Hence this infinite fraternity of feeling…when the big hearts strike together, the concussion is a little stunning.

Farewell…I shall leave the world, I feel, with more satisfaction for having come to know you. Knowing you persuades me more than the Bible of our immortality. [30]

When big hearts strike together, the concussion is a little stunning. Hawthorne and Melville: thunder, lightning, mountains ringing with poetry and a shared, triumphant baptism of immortality, dipped in churning rivers of ink.

SALEM NAVIGATES THE TIDES OF REFORM: ABOLITION AND SLAVERY

N.Y. Times, *Aug. 8, 1859, NEWS BY TELEGRAPH.*
THE SLAVE-TRADE.
Slavers Fitting Out at Salem, Mass.—Where are the Officers of the Government?

Special Dispatch to the New-York Times.
BOSTON, Sunday, Aug. 7
There are at this time two vessels fitting out at Salem, in this State, for the Slave-trade on the coast of Africa. The principals in the affair [are a Spanish] *firm in New-York; and the pecuniary equipment of the vessels has just been forwarded in the form of nearly $20,000 in hard specie. If the Government really wishes to stop this infamous trade it must look North as well as South, and to these small New England ports as well as to New York and New-Orleans. There will be no difficulty in identifying the craft at Salem, and this is not the first instance in the last three months.*

July 30, 1619, marked an important date in freedom with the introduction of representative government: the opening of Virginia's General Assembly.

Ironically, in August 1619, another date must be marked: the first Africans arrived in English America.

A Dutch man-of-war and an English ship out of Jamestown attacked a Portuguese slave ship sailing from Angola to Mexico while it traveled through the West Indies. As a result of this piracy by the two ships, a group of fifty Angolans, which included children, were sent to Jamestown where "20-and-odd" of the African captives were purchased.

These first African captives were quite possibly treated as indentured servants. Historians speculate that they may have been able to buy their freedom after years of working, most likely in the tobacco fields.

By the 1640s, slavery had taken firm root in the soil of the American colonies, north and south. Native Americans, blacks, and whites were enslaved from the time of the earliest European settlement in Massachusetts until slavery itself was abolished by law.

Yet the business of slave trading—which contributed to building many Massachusetts and Salem fortunes and served as the basis on which so many prominent names were elevated to influence and power in the country—continued regardless of those laws.

Salem Navigates the Tides of Reform: Abolition & Slavery

Salem navigated some choppy waters here at home as well as abroad, but came through safely to port at last. *Courtesy of author.*

Samuel Maverick (circa 1602–1676), of Noddle's Island, is considered the first slaveholder in Massachusetts, which commenced sometime between 1624 and 1630.

Captured Native Americans were enslaved in Puritan Massachusetts under confident biblical justifications by their captors. John Winthrop—who landed on Salem's shores, founded Boston and proclaimed the colony's goal to be a moral beacon to humankind—and his relatives owned slaves. He also took active part in the dispersal of enslaved peoples.

Winthrop recorded in his journal in 1638 that the Salem ship *Desire*, which was built in Marblehead, bore "some cotton, and tobacco, and negroes, etc., from thence" after traveling for seven months in the West Indies.

The *Desire* had carried captives taken in the Pequot War to the West Indies, where they were sold as slaves to finance the return trip of the ship with this material and supply a presumably more tractable labor force.

Emmanuel Downing, a Salem settler and brother-in-law to Governor Winthrop, spoke approvingly of waging "Just warre" with the Native Americans. Downing's express goal was to capture and enslave prisoners and, even more importantly, to engage in the slave trade.

This, he said, would be needed to supply "a stock of slaves suffitient to doe all our business [*sic*]." In a 1645 letter to Winthrop, he said that if "the Lord should deliver them into our hands wee might easily have men, woemen and children enough to exchange for Moores…And I suppose you know verie well how wee shall maynteyne 20 Moores cheaper then one Englishe servant [*sic*]." [31]

In 1644, Massachusetts traders began to enter the business of direct importation of slaves from Africa, competing with larger corporate trading bodies such as the Dutch West India Company and the English Royal African Company. Although success at first was limited, New Englanders increased their involvement, building to a level of profitable investment that would become firmly established by 1700. In the eighteenth century, it became serious business.

Salem Slaves and Slavers

The involvement of Salem slaves Tituba and John Indian in the witch hysteria of the late 1600s is commonly known.

In 1718, Salem merchant Colonel Samuel Browne obtained huge tracts of land in Maine, Massachusetts and Lyme, Connecticut. The latter was christened New Salem Parish. He rented most of it out, but on four thousand acres that he retained for his own use—although he never lived there—Browne constructed a plantation complete with perhaps sixty slaves and an overseer.

His grandson, William, who inherited the plantation, became one of the richest and most influential men in Salem.

William Bentley described him as, "short & of a full habit, and remarkable for large legs" and apparently thought well of him.

A Loyalist, William Browne left for England at the outbreak of the Revolutionary War to later become governor of Bermuda. His land in Salem, Massachusetts, and in Connecticut was confiscated and his slaves eventually may have obtained their freedom. [32]

Haunting echoes of the slaveholding Browne family remained behind. Nathaniel Hawthorne wrote the short tale *Browne's Folly* from the Wayside in August 1860:

But what made the hill particularly interesting to me, were the traces of an old and long-vanished edifice, midway on the curving ridge, and at its highest point. A pre-revolutionary magnate, the representative of a famous old Salem family, had here built himself a pleasure house, on a scale of magnificence, which, combined with its airy site and difficult approach, obtained for it and for the entire hill on which it stood, the traditionally title of 'Browne's Folly.' Whether a folly or no, the house was certainly an unfortunate one.

While still in its glory, it was so tremendously shaken by the earthquake of 1755 that the owner dared no longer reside in it; and practically acknowledging that its ambitious site rendered it indeed a Folly, he proceeded to locate it on humbler ground. The great house actually took up its march along the declining ridge of the hill, and came safely to the bottom, where it stood till within the memory of men now alive.

The proprietor, meanwhile, had adhered to the Royalist side, and fled to England during the Revolution. The mansion was left under the care of Richard Derby (an ancestor of the present Derby family), who had a claim to the Browne property through his wife, but seems to have held the premises precisely as the refugee left them, for a long term of years, in the expectation of his eventual return. The house remained, with all its furniture in its spacious rooms and chambers, ready for the exile's occupancy, as soon as he should reappear. As time went on, however, it began to be neglected, and was accessible to whatever vagrant, or idle school-boy, or berrying party might choose to enter through its illsecured windows.

But there was one closet in the house, which everybody was afraid to enter, it being supposed that an evil spirit—perhaps a domestic Demon of the Browne family—was confined in it.[33]

Cambridge, a Negro Man belonging to James Oliver of Boston doth absent himself sometimes from his Master: said Negro plays well upon a flute, and not so well on a Violin…All Masters of Vessels are also forbid to have anything to do with him on any Account, as they may answer it in the Law. N.B. Said Negro is to be sold: Enquire of said Oliver.
—Boston Evening Post, *October 24, 1743*

In July 1629, an indentured servant with the Massachusetts Bay Colony Company, William Riall or Ryall [*sic*] (circa 1580–1676) arrived in Salem, Massachusetts, on the *Lion's Whelp*. After serving his time, he received a land grant in Maine but eventually moved to Dorchester, Massachusetts, in

1675. He and his wife, Phebe Green, had several children, including William Royall, father of Isaac Royall Sr. (1672–1739).

In Medford, slave quarters still remain and can be visited on the Isaac Royall Sr. estate. He purchased the six-hundred-acre Ten Hills Farm in 1732—including land on which John Winthrop had resided—and moved there with more than twenty slaves after building his wealth through trading in West Indian rum, lumber, dried fish and slaves.[34]

From 1740 to 1769, the slave trade flourished in New England, with Boston and Newport, Rhode Island, serving as major ports for slave ships. Salem merchants and shipowners were active participants in the slave trade, and slaves were owned within Salem as well.

In 1760, Boston-born Timothy Fitch took as a second wife Salem widow Eunice Brown Plaisted. The family maintained homes in Boston, Medford and Salem. After his marriage to Eunice, Fitch, who was a merchant, became involved in the slave trade, as evidenced by letters he wrote to captains onboard his ships. He owned several ships, including the *Snow Caesar* and a schooner called the *Charming Phyllis*. According to the Medford Historical Society, Fitch's ships "were directly involved in the trade and trafficking of slaves from Africa."[35]

In her discussion of the slave trade after the Revolutionary War, scholar Elizabeth Donnan found that "the most active of the Massachusetts ports was not Boston but Salem, which, somewhat slow to enter the trade, was reluctant to relinquish it."[36]

In his survey of Boston slave for-sale ads in the 1700s, Robert E. Desrochers describes a *Boston Gazette* story of 1733 recounting "the story of a slave woman in Salem, who…enacted what appears to have been an African-inspired graveside reincarnation ritual. 'Determined to go into her own Country,' as she call'd it, the woman 'took a Bottle of Rum & two Biskets…into the Burying Place…where she dug a hole & and cover'd em' before taking her own life with a knife."[37]

Scholars commonly point to Joseph B. Felt's *Annals of Salem* for references to slaves and slave trading.

At this time there were 2,000 slaves, including a few Indians, in Massachusetts…Of their number, in 1754, being about 4,489 for the Commonwealth, Salem had 47 males and 36 females of 16 years old and above…under such an age would make 34 additional, and the total 117….

Benjamin Alford, of Boston, who had been a slave in Barbary, and William Bowditch, of Salem, state that their friend Robert Carver, also of this place, was taken nine years before, 'a captive into Sally,' that contributions had been made for his redemption."[38]

William Bentley's journal makes many allusions to slave-trading merchants and sea captains. In 1789, he wrote of "News of the death of Captain William Fairfield, who commanded the schooner which sailed in Capt. Jo White's employ in the African Slave Trade. He was killed by the Negroes on board."

The spectacular arrest of the slave-trading career of the "daring wretch" John Sinclair is recounted with some relish in 1792. In 1793, he reported the death of Captain Spence Hall, who died "in the Guinea Trade," and the death of another captain in the same line of work not long after.

In 1802, Bentley writes, "The company of Prince, G. Ropes, & Philips of this Town have been questioned by the government upon complaint of the Slave Trade...Of the facts there is no question but in what degree & upon what evidence we do not know. We know men will do anything for money."

According to scholars who have done extensive research in the history of slavery in New England, in 1788, Captain George Crowninshield sent his ships *Polly* and *Sally* to Africa for slaves. In addition to Crowninshield, Salem's Benjamin Hathorne; Joseph Waters; Gedney Clarke Sr., who was based in Barbados; and Joseph and Joshua Grafton also derived wealth from the traffic in slaves.

Ownership of slaves was largely concentrated "in the commercial and industrial counties of Suffolk, Essex, and Plymouth." (The 1771 census shows where slaves resided in Salem.)

In 1641, Massachusetts was the first colony to legally sanction slavery. Although not the first state to abolish the practice, the Massachusetts constitution of 1780 contained a clause that was later interpreted as a prohibition of slavery. With landmark court cases, particularly one under chief justice William Cushing in 1783, the turning of the legal tide against slavery began in earnest.

A timeline published online in 2008 by the U.S. Coast Guard described the oncoming antislave-trading wave:

March 22nd, 1794: Congress declared that no American citizen may carry slaves from the U.S. to another nation or between foreign nations.

Jan 1st, 1808: Importation of slaves into the U.S. was declared illegal. Congress charged the Revenue Cutter Service with enforcing the law on the high seas.

May 15th, 1820: Congress declared the foreign slave trade to be piracy and instituted the death penalty for any U.S. citizen engaged in the slave trade.

Other countries too, most notably England, began active policing of the seas by pursuing and seizing slavers.

But enforcement proved extremely problematic. Fortunes had been built and maintained on the lucrative lure of human trafficking. Slave labor bought, sold and utilized was thoroughly interwoven into the economic fabric of maritime communities. Ships became adept at hiding the purpose of their mission.

In Calvin Lane's online discussion of the U.S. Navy's role in policing the slave trade, he wrote: "If a U.S. Navy vessel chased what seemed to be a slaver its ostensible 'captain' would hoist the Spanish flag, substitute Spanish registration papers, and might even carry a Spanish crew hidden below decks. This stratagem would be exactly reversed if apprehended by a British man of war."

Yet, under these conditions the trade flourished…with an estimated one thousand per year smuggled into the United States…from 1807 to the Civil War.

Commercial ties between legitimate maritime trade and the slave trade further complicated the problem. American merchant ships carried rum, tobacco, flour and cloth to trade along the bulge of Africa for palm oil, gum copal, ivory, gold dust and peanuts. Enoch Ware, a trading agent aboard the Salem brig *Northumberland*, gloated after arriving on the coast ahead of his competitors:

Now if no envious competitor present himself the prospect could not be well better—that is if my Sierra Leone tobacco will suit for the slave trade. No! What am I to know for what purpose it is to be sold? I sell for produce or money. The use of it afterwards certainly am not accountable for…scarcely a hundred pounds of Tobacco or Powder that is sold but what sooner or later is used for purchasing slaves though it may go through half a dozen hands first.[39]

Horrific tales—documented—also abound of captains cruelly throwing their human captives overboard if seizure looked unavoidable.

As you, Gentle Reader, may see from the August 8, 1859 *New York Times* article quoted at the beginning of this section, slave-trading ships were "fitted out" in Salem right to the very eve of the Civil War.

Seized by the hair and with a glove and cloth shoved into his mouth to prevent his speaking, the life of Christopher Holder would have surely been choked off had not Samuel Shattuck stepped forward at the Salem meeting to release him.

Shattuck was a member of a band of Quakers who had been meeting at the house of Lawrence and Cassandra Southwick in defiance of the increasingly severe prohibitions against the practice of their religion instituted by the governing Puritans. Holder had attempted to speak, guided by his beliefs, after the sermon at the Puritan meeting.

The reaction was predictable.

The Quakers faced great oppression in early Salem and Massachusetts. *From Samuel Adams Drake and F.T. Merrill's* A Book of New England Legends and Folk Lore in Prose and Poetry.

By 1658, when fining, imprisonment, examinations for witchcraft or ear-cropping and tongue-boring with hot irons had not prevented Quakers from testifying about the Inner Light, things got tougher; here was yet another law: Quakers were now to be banished or suffer execution.

The little Salem group was disbanded; members were fined and deported.

The Southwicks, who were elderly, died in exile on Shelter Island. When their children proved unable to pay the fines levied against their parents, they were put up for sale into slavery. Only the refusal of shipmasters to transport them prevented this dire result.[40]

In 1688, the Quakers of Germantown, Pennsylvania, issued the first officially promulgated antislavery statement in the world. At this time, Quakers owned slaves and were participants in the slave trade but, after the declaration, antislavery conviction grew among the Friends. They helped form the world's first abolitionist society in Philadelphia in April 1775; by 1784, the last slaves held by Quakers were freed.

New England

Before the American Revolution, there was no great social stigma attached to owning slaves in the colonies and participation in the slave trade was part of a worldwide commercial norm. American colonists were no exception to that norm.

In New England, slaves were usually referred to as servants, and with this designation came an entire array of socially sanctioned attitudes and behaviors toward those held in bondage. But with the ideas of the Age of Enlightenment and the rhetoric of freedom engendered by the Revolutionary War, the issue of slavery began to be reexamined.

Framing the Big Picture

It is important to discuss upfront the fact that the term antislavery covers a very broad spectrum of attitudes, activity and convictions throughout our discussion. Antislavery sentiments, or even public avowals of support for antislavery ideals, were not automatically synonymous with abolitionist activism.

To believe that slavery was a system to be eliminated might mean you believed it to be economically necessary and even to be beneficial for the slave, but perhaps you also expected that slavery would die a natural death as the colonies grew in strength and native population.

Or you might have believed it was a moral outrage against God and humankind that must be rooted out of the country, if necessary, and immediately abolished, even if with violence.

If you were a slave, your own understanding and accommodation to the realities of your existence also could be located anywhere on a continuum: choosing death, resistance, flight, or submission. Eventually, former slaves chose personal and communal political activism.

Between extreme methods in any reform movement lies an entire landscape of legal, moral, social, and religious paths to take.

Political Stepping Stones

In 1774, Connecticut and Rhode Island prohibited further importation of slaves; in 1777, the Vermont constitution prohibited slavery. Pennsylvania granted gradual emancipation in 1780, followed, again, by Connecticut and Rhode Island and later New York and New Jersey. The Massachusetts constitution contained a clause that allowed for later legal interpretation as a prohibition against slavery. The U.S. Constitution compromised on the issue of slavery, apportioning a fractional humanity to the slave and declaring the slave trade must end two decades later.

Behind each of these political and legal steps and the ones that followed swirled a world of controversy and evolving attitudes, leading, eventually, to the cataclysmic American Civil War. These events and attitudes left an enduring residue of challenges in our society to this day.

An All-Too-Human Story

The antislavery-reform movement is a long tale of greed, morality, corruption, heroism, confusion, conviction, integrity, churlishness, racism, enlightenment, tolerance, unbridled capitalism, and revulsion against same.

It's a tale of the rule of law, the "law of the jungle" and of indifference and agitation. The Second Great Awakening of the late 1820s through the 1830s added religious energy, including fervent evangelical notes, to the mix.

The antislavery movement was embedded and utilized in national political struggles. With the election of Thomas Jefferson, New England's Federalist power base looked with dismay at the decline of their national political dominance. The fear of losing elite status and power motivated many and accounted for injection of a stridently moralistic edge into the debate. Sectional differences fueled by this development would burst into angry prominence.

The Hartford Convention of 1814–15, which gave a platform to antislavery rhetoric and in which prominent Salemites participated, also set a precedent for the concept of secession from the Union.

The antislavery movement embodied conscious struggle for sectional cultural dominance. The prevailing social order in all aspects was challenged, including gender issues, the place of artists in societal change, concepts of racial differences, economic class structure and labor issues. And all of this took place within a larger global context.

The compromises accepted in the adoption of the U.S. Constitution, including those that regarded slavery, engendered a subsequent journey through legal questions, challenges, and rulings. In so doing, it fostered the growth and power of the U.S. judicial process in ways that resonate still.

An excellent example of the complexity of these constitutional issues is provided by studying Marblehead's own Supreme Court justice Joseph Story, who was born in 1779. Story opened his law office in Salem in 1801 and was the first lawyer to publicly declare himself in Federalist Essex County as a Jeffersonian Republican. A man personally against slavery, he yet maintained a professional constitutional stance throughout his career that serves to highlight the complexity of the issue.

No short section such as this can do justice to the entire sweep of the antislavery movement, but keep this background firmly in mind as we move on.

Father of Mercy! befriend the opprest; At the voice of thy Gospel of Peace, May the sorrows of Africa cease; And the Slave and his Master devoutly unite, To walk in thy freedom and dwell in thy light.
—*"The Slave Trade,"* Salem Gazette, *December 10, 1819*

To the Right Honourable the Lords Spiritual and Temporal of Great Britain, in Parliament assembled.
The PETITION of the SHARKS of AFRICA
Sheweth, THAT your petitioners are a numerous body, and at present in a very flourishing situation, owing chiefly to the constant visitation of the shipping of your island.
That by hovering round these floating dungeons, your petitioners are supplied with large quantities of their most favourite food—human flesh.
That your petitioners are sustained, not only by the carcases[sic] of those who have fallen by distempers, but are frequently gratified with rich repasts from the bodies of living negroes who voluntarily plunge into the

abodes of your petitioners, preferring instant destruction by their jaws, to the imaginary horrors of a lingering slavery
—Historical Register or Edinburgh Monthly Intelligencer, *May 1792*

Scotsman James Tytler came to America and landed in Salem in August 1795 as a political refugee. The quote above is from his satirical broadside, which was, according to scholar Marcus Rediker (who uncovered it) "republished widely, in Edinburgh, Philadelphia, New York, and Salem."[41]

Most antebellum antislavery activity focused on abolishing the slave trade itself, with the expectation that over time, without fresh supplies of slaves, slavery would die out. After passage of the Federal Slave Trade Act in March 1794 and the 1808 Slave Trade Act, it was unlawful to outfit a ship for the slave trade or to import slaves into the United States. Ironically, Eli Whitney patented the cotton gin on March 14, 1794, which made slave labor all the more economically important.

That no citizen or citizens of the United States, or any other person, shall, from and after the first day of January, in the year of our Lord one thousand eight hundred and eight, for himself, or themselves, or any other person whatsoever, either as master, factor, or owner, build, fit, equip, load or otherwise prepare any ship or vessel…for the purpose of procuring any negro, mulatto, or person of colour, from any foreign kingdom, place, or country, to be transported…within the jurisdiction of the United States, to be held, sold, or disposed of as slaves, or to be held to service or labor.—1808 Slave Trade Act

The laws were difficult to enforce, and commercial interests scorned even the ethics of the matter. As we have seen, Salem merchants and shipmasters outfitted ships for the slave trade right to the eve of the Civil War.

Salem Steps Up to the Plate

In 1619, the first slaves were landed in Virginia. Two hundred years later, in 1819, political tides were turning, building strength for a wave of reform that would sweep the United States into a redefinition of its nationhood.

The great catalyst for the New England and Northern movement toward the active abolition of slavery was inherently political in the expansion of slavery into the territories, which heightened a long-standing struggle for sectionalist power balances between North, South and West. This struggle was escalated by the progressive admission of new states to the Union.

A financial panic, the most serious to date, also gripped the country in 1819, adding to the underlying tension.

With the petition of the slaveholding territory of Missouri in 1818 for statehood, tension became crisis; the balance of slave states versus free states was threatened. An amendment to ban slavery in Missouri was proposed in February 1819 by Representative James Tallmadge, of New York. The resulting Missouri Question consumed the country.

A well-attended convention in New York in November 1819 issued a manifesto that said slavery "was a great political, as well as moral evil." On the morning of December 7, 1819, Salem echoed the cry.

In precise and elegant penmanship is recorded the sentiments of "the Inhabitants of the town of Salem qualified to vote" who met at this "Spec'l" meeting to discuss the "Subject of Slavery."

> *Resolved, That in the opinion of this meeting, it is the duty of the people and Government of the United States, by all practicable means to prevent the extension of so great a political and mortal evil as Slavery; and for this end, that it is constitutional and expedient to prohibit the introduction of it into such States as may hereafter be established in any territory of the United States, without the original limits of the said States.*[42]

At this meeting, Judge Joseph Story "closed the discussion in a speech of great ability and interest, in the course of a most conclusive and elaborate argument; in which he examined all the clauses of the Constitution" and "demonstrated the Constitutionality of excluding Slavery from Missouri."

All resolutions passed during the "uncommonly numerous and respectable meeting" were reported to have passed unanimously.

Two Salem abolitionist societies were local chapters of the American Anti-Slavery Society, which was organized by William Lloyd Garrison. Membership was drawn from Salem and surrounding towns. Cyrus P. Grosvenor was president in 1834 and 1835 and was pastor of Salem's Central Baptist Church.

His wife was president of the sister organization, the Salem Female Anti-Slavery Society, reorganized in 1834. (The first Female Anti-Slavery Society was formed in Salem in 1832 by African Americans.) According to the scholarship of Beth A. Salerno, there were some 230 female antislavery societies in the United States between 1832 and 1859.[43]

Interestingly, according to the organizational notes, the men's society discussed interpretations of constitutional and legal ideals while, at the women's initial meeting, the notes show they stressed moral values and even described the shared humanity of all.

> *Formation and Constitution of the Anti-Slavery Society of Salem and Vicinity, Commenced January 2, 1834*
>
> *I. The Object*
> *Our object is the extinction of Slavery in the Nation of which we are citizens.*
> *II. The Motives*
> *Our first motive is the unmerited sufferings of our fellow men, who are held in slavery under the laws of several of the states of this Union.*
>
> *These sufferings consist in their deprivation of Liberty and its concomitant blessings, as they are enjoyed by the Free under the Constitution and laws of this nation…We believe the truths which, in the Declaration of our Independence are solemnly asserted as "Self-evident."*
> —*Constitution of the Salem Female Anti-Slavery Society, June 4, 1834*

> *Whereas it is our belief, that the principle upon which all Slavery is founded, viz: that man may, in some cases, innocently hold property in man, is a false principle.*
>
> *And whereas we are fully convinced that the system based upon it is subversive of every precept of christianity, and hostile to the best interests of all who are under its influence;—causing unjust and oppressive distinctions in the human family;—injuring the morals and tending to destroy all the kind and noble affections of one class, and blotting out from the other, as far as the most systematic degradation can do it,—the impress of the divine image.*
>
> *3d. It is a duty, rested upon us, to endeavor, constantly, to elevate the condition of this class of people among ourselves; and to show that we do not consider them a distinct and lower caste, on account of their color;—but that we are ready to acknowledge them as friends and equals.*

Salemites included freeborn black business people, lecturers and activists. Among the best known are Salem's Remond family. Their home became a vital Salem meeting place for those involved in the antislavery cause. Sarah Parker Remond (1826–1894) and her brother, Charles Lenox Remond (1810–1873), were born in Salem and educated in the town's public schools. They became highly successful lecturers in the abolitionist cause.

Charles became the first black representative of the American Anti-Slavery Society, the movement's first black lecturer and the first black person to address the Massachusetts Legislature. Sarah became a successful and sought-after international public speaker who courageously pushed for civil rights as an African American and as a woman.

And now, in parting, let us at least mention the music. "Slavery would have died of that music, and that response of the multitude."

Ah! But, as to this wondrous song, and those who sang it…Well, Gentle Reader, the clock bids us return another day. We will take up that tuneful story in a future book.

Voices

There is a saying that we shall doe to all men like as we will be done ourselves; making no difference of what generation, descent or colour they are. And those who steal or rob men, and those who buy or purchase them, are they not alike? Here is liberty of conscience wch is right and reasonable; here ought to be likewise liberty of ye body, except of evil-doers, wch is an other case. But to bring men hither, or to rob and sell them against their will, we stand against. [sic]
—the Quaker Germantown Protest, 1688

See your Declaration Americans!!! Do you understand your own language? Hear your languages, proclaimed to the world, July 4th, 1776—"We hold these truths to be self evident—that ALL MEN ARE CREATED EQUAL!! that they are endowed by their Creator with certain unalienable rights; that among these are life, liberty, and the pursuit of happiness!!"
—David Walker's Appeal, *1829*

Beloved Sisters
We are thy sisters—God has truly said,
That of one blood the nations He has made.
Oh, Christian women in a Christian land,
Canst thou unblushing read this great command?
Our skins may differ, but from thee we claim
A sister's privilege, and a sister's name.
—Sarah Forten, quoted in a pamphlet issued by the Anti-Slavery Convention of American Women, 1838

Salem Common. *From C.H. Webber and Winfield S. Nevins's* Old Naumkeag: An Historical Sketch of the City of Salem, and the Towns of Marblehead, Peabody, Beverly, Danvers, Wenham, Manchester, Topsfield, and Middleton.

AM I NOT A MAN AND BROTHER? *Am I not a man and brother? Ought I not, then, to be free? Sell me not one to another, Take not thus my liberty. Christ our Saviour, Christ our Saviour, Died for me as well as thee.*
—*from* The Anti-Slavery Harp, *1848.*

As I would not be a slave, so I would not be a master. This expresses my idea of democracy. Whatever differs from this, to the extent of the difference, is not democracy.
—*Abraham Lincoln, August 1, 1858*

Chapter 2
Culture Then and Now

SALEM'S PSYCHIC PAST LIVES

Softly, softly, hear the rustle
Of the Spirits airy wings;
They are coming down to mingle
Once again with earthly things…
Rap-tap-tap lost friends are near you.
Rap-tap-tap they see and hear you.
—From the 1853 song Spirit Rappings. Words by J. Ellwood Garrett, Esq., and music
by W.W. Rossington

She's smiling in the crude illustration on the tattered flyer and sitting serenely, surrounded by flying guitars, airborne tambourines, floating violins, and disembodied flute players. Yes, she smiles, with long dark tresses tumbling over her right shoulder, although she's been immobilized by "strips of cotton cloth, which are sewn with thread, and further [secured] with court plaster."

"While in this helpless condition," the broadside breathlessly informs us, there will be a "Series of Bewildering Effects," including, among many other wonders, "The Animated Violin…The Mouth Organ in its Travels, The Great Goblet and Water Mystery," all of which, we are assured, were "A puzzle to the scientist; what unseen power produces these results?"

The mysterious manifestations produced at each séance with Miss Fay, promised to those who would come to see the medium at Lyceum Hall that

The Judge Jonathan Corwin house, better known as the Witch House, backed by the outline of a church. It is the only building with direct ties to the Salem witch hysteria. Enough said. *Courtesy of author.*

November evening, were mind-boggling to say the least. For during this rather musical evening with the so-called Indescribable Phenomenon, one could also expect to enjoy a "Religious Illustrated Lecture of Spirit Power in Full Gas Light," with full-form materialization.

And, at the end of her trance, the medium called upon a "self-acting knife" that mysteriously cut her bonds![44]

Nineteenth-century history in the United States is rich and fertile ground for the scholar, particularly those of us whose focus is on the performing arts and manifestations of intellectual, artistic, literary, or religious currents in popular culture. For me, one of the most rewarding historical threads to follow has always been the incredible variety and vigor of religious and social-reform movements that percolated all century long.

At first glance, one might wonder, what do séances like the one I described have to do with religion? Piled on my desk are dozens of similar broadsides and printed ad copies gleaned from archives and libraries; they are nearly all couched in the familiar bombastic language of entertainment. However, it

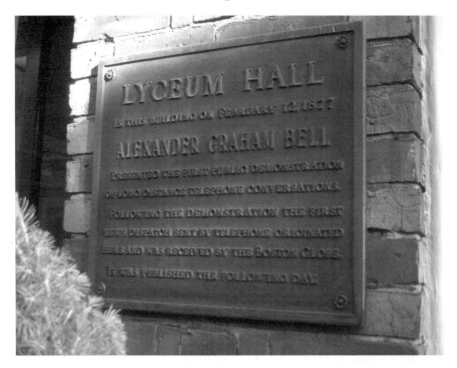

Plaque on the outside of the Lyceum Restaurant, marking its historic past. *Courtesy of author.*

is useful to understand the growth and proliferation of occult disciplines as incubating within the framework of America's religious pluralism.

In particular, it is fascinating to study the forms that grew from what Sydney Ahlstrom has termed "the unconventional currents streaming through the many levels of American religion during the antebellum half-century."[45] Some of those currents flowed initially from Europe, yet took on a peculiarly American flavor and vitality all their own, upon transplantation.

All the occult disciplines have deep historical roots. Of course in Salem, Andover, and Danvers, we have a rather active and current awareness of early colonists' belief in the occult; the witchcraft hysteria is only one manifestation of this belief. We should also remember practices, historically, to command occult forces in native cultures and in communities of the unlettered and enslaved.

Currents from late eighteenth and early nineteenth century Western Europe subsequently influential in America included the sweeping and comprehensive religious teachings of Emanuel Swedenborg (1688–1772), the theories of animal magnetism propounded by Franz (Friedrich) Mesmer (1734–1815), a cornucopia of secret societies, and phrenology.

After 1848, America was flooded by Spiritualism. By the 1880s, popular movements included theosophy and scientific research of psychic phenomena. After 1893, especially due to the World Parliament of Religions, there was growing interest in Asian religions; through the turn of the twentieth century, there was renewed interest in ritual magic and divination, and so on into the twentieth century, when the occult saturation of popular culture gave rise to mass-market astrology advice in newspapers after the 1930s.

Spiritualism

In 1848, two young citizens of western New York sparked a spiritual wildfire. In the spring of that year, "spirit rappings" began to fill the lives of Hydesville sisters Margaret and Katherine Fox. Their neighbors became enraptured by the girls' development of mediumistic achievements: "communications from the dead, table tippings, spirit writing and materialization." The rapture was to overtake the entire country as Spiritualism.

Spiritualism's rapid growth was helped mightily by the conversion of the *New York Weekly Tribune*'s Horace Greely. Friendly publicity followed the Fox sisters' plunge into commercial séances in 1849. Older sister Leah, with her Rochester music classes disrupted by the rapping following Kate's arrival

This March 28, 1843 ad from the *Salem Gazette* says it all. Note the laudable achievements of the dog. *Courtesy of author.*

in her home, eventually joined the two girls in their public demonstrations. Many other mediums followed in their wake.

Spiritualism, with its declaration of the immortality of the spirit and comforting answers to the awesome mystery of death, spread to England and the European continent as well.

Of course, the sideshow element of Spiritualism was pronounced. Serious adherents to Spiritualism as a religious movement, however, evolved a doctrine that addressed theological, scientific, medical, and societal issues.

Spiritualist activities did not merely include the work of mediums in séances and public demonstrations. The movement produced serious lectures, books, journals, and music. One of the most important Spiritualist journals was local—the *Boston Banner of Light*—and, in Boston, Spiritualists developed a "fairly stable and respected denominational status."

The Salem Seer: Charles H. Foster

In a compiled listing of those who, in the 1880 federal census, identified their occupation as "clairvoyant, spirit medium, psychometrist, trance lecturer, magnetic healer" or other "professional spiritualist or occultist," there are well over five hundred names. Three were listed in Salem: Sophia Cross, Irving W. Glidden and Charles H. Harding. I've turned up more practitioners through various ads, ephemera collections, theatre programs, and archival sources throughout the nineteenth century and well into the twentieth. Yet the most famous, perhaps, of all our homegrown spiritualistic practitioners, was the Salem Seer, Charles H. Foster.

Sir Arthur Conan Doyle, an enthusiastic Spiritualist who became president of the College of Psychic Studies, Fédération Spirites Internationale, the London Spiritualist Alliance, and author of a two-volume History of Spiritualism wrote about Foster:

> *Charles H. Foster is fortunate in having a biographer who was such an admirer that he called him "the greatest spiritual medium since Swedenborg." There is a tendency on the part of writers to exaggerate the claims of the particular sensitive with whom they have been brought in contact. None the less, Mr. George C. Bartlett in his "The Salem Seer" shows that he had close personal acquaintance with Foster, and that he really was a very remarkable medium. His fame was not confined to America, for he traveled widely and visited both Australia and Great Britain. In the latter country*

Salem's very own marvelous Seer, Charles H. Foster. *From the frontispiece to* The Salem Seer: Reminiscences of Charles H. Foster *by George C. Bartlett.*

he made friends with Bulwer Lytton, visited Knebworth, and became the original of Margrave in "A Strange Story."

Foster seems to have been a clairvoyant of great power, and had the peculiar gift of being able to bring out the name or initials of the spirit which he described upon his own skin, usually upon his forearm. This phenomenon was so often repeated and so closely examined that there can be no possible doubt as to the fact.[46]

George Bartlett's little book on Foster, and archival copies of his 1873 *Voices from the Press: All About Charles H. Foster, the Wonderful Medium,* makes for fascinating reading; the accounts of individual séances are particularly lively and sometimes unintentionally amusing. Mr. Foster was, as they say, "quite a card."

Naumkeag Notations

Foster died on December 15, 1885 (comforted by the "spirits who had been helped by him"), and is buried in Harmony Grove Cemetery in Salem. His previous fifty-two years had been a wild ride of séances (fees raised from two to five dollars upon meeting Mr. Bartlett), spirit writings arising from his very skin, exhausting visions of truly terrible deaths and subsequent comforting of the bereaved. His dual nature, as Bartlett described it, would enable him to sit in séances for days and nights on end and then, not surprisingly, "days and weeks would come when he would turn hundreds of dollars away and disappoint the people" and "do absolutely nothing."

Foster sat for Emperor Napoleon and his empress, Belgium's King Leopold, Robert Browning, Walt Whitman, Alfred Lord Tennyson, and Mary Todd Lincoln. (Mrs. Lincoln went "beyond all bounds" in her interest and belief in Spiritualism, writes Bartlett, snippishly.) Foster was "often visited by musical people," having been "very intimate with Louis Gottschalk and Ole Bull," among other famous musicians.

Foster kept a summer home in Salem. His family of origin continued here while "Charlie" careened through the circuit. Mr. Foster, senior, was a kind and pleasing man, who in his youth had "followed the sea." Both parents told Bartlett they, too, had conversed quite naturally with spirits all their lives—Charlie, in fact, had been rocked in the cradle by spirit friends who aided his overworked mother.

At his death, a eulogist opined that Foster was "sensitive to his every surrounding, and might fitly be compared to an Aeolian [sic] harp, which responds at once to every breeze."

In Salem, as in America as a whole, that psychic tune still ripples today. In 2006, there were eleven licensed individual fortunetellers and four fortunetelling stores in Salem. Each fortunetelling store can have up to five licenses for store employees engaged in fortunetelling. Two of the stores had the maximum of five employees and the other two stores had three employees.

Salem only allows four fortunetelling stores and five fortunetelling licenses, although some are grandfathered in.

Psychic Healers

Friend!

You say you're sore oppressed?

Perhaps your trouble is catarrh, or neurasthenia. You're going deaf, you suffer "biliousness," your knees are stiff; you're fatigued, depressed, you suffer dyspepsia, insomnia, liver troubles. You have—uh—female troubles. You might not even know what's wrong with you but, oh, you suffer so.

Come, friend; let's peel back the veil of time and space; consult the newspapers with me; then get your cloak, and let us take a little stroll back into the nineteenth century to survey Salem's psychic landscape.

At 141 Essex Street is the permanent office of Chief Wia. He tells us he is "the only natural born and living Real Indian Medicine Man in Salem." "You don't need to say a word to Chief Wia…He does not feel you or touch any part to locate ailments. Chief Wia is not a spiritualist…but he looks into the body, locates the aches and pains, and feels within himself all of your troubles."

We've seen his frequent, attractive advertisements. We are assured that he affects "many great cures" and assails "strange cases successfully after the best doctors have failed." "The whole world…says: well he is a wonder." "Thousands of people in Salem" have benefited from his amazing powers, which include being surveyed by his "left eye, which is a perfect X-Ray."

The great American Indian specialist keeps regular hours, with free consultations, at his laboratory office. There he mixes miraculous medicines derived from roots, barks and herbs and imbues it with his "good power" as he hands it to his patient. Walk-ins are also welcome across the street at his private office. Local doctors harbor the "very best of feeling" toward Chief Wia since they are delighted he can cure where they cannot.

Next stop: 81 Washington Street, Room 5, where Healer Dennis, ensconced in Salem "since 1890," keeps his office. Using the Dennis System of Vital Magnetism, he cures the sick at Lynde Street Chapel (for free) every Tuesday, but we can consult him privately on Tuesdays, Wednesdays, Fridays, and Saturdays from 9:00 a.m. to 4:00 p.m. "Life and Health Come at the Magic Touch of Healer Dennis."

After eighteen years in Salem, he's cured "Appendicitis, Sciatica, Rheumatism, Hiccoughs, Dispepsia, [*sic*] Neuralgia…all Stomach Troubles, Blindness, Heart Trouble, Nervous Prostration, Lost Voice Restored, St. Vitus Dance, all forms of Paralysis…No Drugs, No Operations, but Wonderful Cures."

Unfortunately, Healer Dennis has had to oppose reports that he is "down on" regular doctors. "Hate forms no part of his creed but he rises…in righteous indignation upon those who invade his natural rights and seek through envy and malice to injure a man whose work is of great value to mankind."

The Essex House, where visiting folks stayed and, apparently, quite a magnet for those in need of healing. *From C.H. Webber and Winfield S. Nevins's* Old Naumkeag: An Historical Sketch of the City of Salem, and the Towns of Marblehead, Peabody, Beverly, Danvers, Wenham, Manchester, Topsfield, and Middleton.

Let's move on. This modest classified ad steers us to 10 Conant Street, where you can consult a Business Medium who will give us private sittings and Magnetic Treatments.

Or, if you prefer, Professor A.D. Fritz will read disease and examine our case through "Psychic-Power." He promises to heal by "scientific application of 'Magnetism or the 'Divine Power.'" He gives a test of his abilities every Monday and Thursday at 138 Essex Street and is successful because "he possesses the scientific requirements with experience…gifted from childhood with intuitive genius."

Dr. C. Blake Gridley performs "marvelous cures daily" at Boston's Magnopathic Medical Institute. He'll be at Essex House in Salem on successive Wednesdays, starting March 18, 1891. By the "laying on of hands," he'll cure "any disease to which the flesh is heir." He is, we are assured, no "uneducated or unlearned Quack, but a regularly qualified and perfectly experienced Magnetic Healer."

What's Going on Here?

The transplanted animal magnetism theories of Franz Anton Mesmer had, by the middle of the nineteenth century in America, solidified claims of scientific validity for practitioners and their largely middle-class clientele— while simultaneously evolving integral spiritual and religious components.

"Each stage in the mesmerizing process was thought to correspond to a successively deeper level of the mind," noted Robert C. Fuller in *Mesmerism and the American Cure of Souls*.[47] Those stages incorporated hypnotic trance and could culminate, according to American mesmerists, in a "final stage of lucidity or clairvoyant wisdom…subjects feel themselves to be united with the creative principle of the universe."

"Mesmerism," writes Fuller, "promised to help its adherents transcend the affairs of mundane existence and experience ecstatic states of consciousness and paranormal mental powers."

That the rise of mesmerism in the United States coincided, during the 1830s, with the high-water mark of the Second Great Awakening helped propel the movement toward its peculiarly American form. The influence of mesmerism seeped throughout American culture, with references to it surfacing even in literary works by Emerson, Hawthorne, and Edgar Allan Poe.

Occult Oracles

Claims of healing abilities were also routinely listed alongside the "paranormal mental powers" of professional oracles: seers, clairvoyants, fortunetellers, and even stage magicians.

Madame Leone, "The Wonder of the World" and "Clairvoyant and Medium, Born With A Veil," holding forth at Higbee House at 150 Washington Street, claimed cures of "Rheumatism of long standing, Sprains, Female Weakness, Neuralgia, Weak Lungs, and Deafness, etc…by her mysterious power."

Yet her stated main stock in trade was psychic consultations on "Love, Business, Absent Friends, Sickness, Theft. Causes Speedy Marriages…tells your very thoughts on entering the house…gives luck and numbers."

Madame claimed oracular fame for solving the Proctor murder in Salem, finding missing persons and predicting the outcomes of upcoming presidential elections. Those weren't bad returns for fees ranging from fifty cents to one dollar "and upwards."

For consultation on "all the affairs of life," one could also patronize the "young, popular and celebrated Clairvoyant" Lotta J. Darling, who in successive visits to Salem took parlors at 23 Summer Street and Higbee House. A mind-numbing avalanche of advertising materials, including truly execrable poetry, accompanied the lady's visits. All were urged to "consult her, as she is the most reliable medium that has ever visited this place."

She was confident enough to issue a "$1,000 challenge! To any Astrologer or Medium to excel her in her startling revelations of the past, present, and future events of one's life." (As if this were not enough, her "Fattening

An optimistic Salemite.
Courtesy of author.

Remedy, Blood Purifier, Appetizer, and Beautifier" also promised "Beauty! Beauty! Beauty!")

Yet she too made it a point to attribute her powers to the spiritual realm. "Clergymen acknowledge genuineness…Spiritualists are intoxicated with delight."

Musical Sprits

With the mention of Spiritualism we come full circle. I'll leave you with just a snippet of "musical spirits" to close our psychic tour.

"Spiritualist séances sometimes featured invisible spirit instrumentalists producing sounds from floating trumpets, drums, guitars, or pianos. At a séance at P. T. Barnum's hotel in New York, for example, William Lloyd Garrison, William Cullen Bryant, and Horace Greeley…were visited by the spirit of recently-deceased spiritualist, singer and impressario of the Hutchinson Family Singers, Jesse Hutchinson, who levitated a guitar and tambourine and played Jesse's popular tune, 'The Old Granite State,' according to John B. Buescher, author of *The Other Side of Salvation: Spiritualism in the Nineteenth-Century Religious Experience*.

Jesse Hutchinson Jr., who had performed in Salem several times with his singing family in the antebellum years, came to Spiritualism due to the devastating loss of all of his children and his wife, Susanna. He kept a home at Old High Rock in Lynn, a site with a history of connection with the paranormal and that became somewhat of a spiritualist sanctuary during Jesse's tenure. Before he died of a fever in 1853, Jesse lent his name to the movement in some surprising ways.

For instance, the song *The Haunted Ground*, published in 1851, bore a picture of the Fox family on the cover. Beneath the picture the cover reads, "Words by the late Mrs. Hemens, Music from the spirit land. affectionately dedicated to the friends of spiritual progress and reform. By Jesse Hutchinson."

Some of the lyrics, reportedly dictated to Leah from the other world, serve as a fitting cap to our visit to Salem's ever-present psychic past:

> *Away away! that my soul may soar*
> *As a free bird of the blue skies once more!*
> *Here from its wing it may never cast*
> *The chain by those spirits brought back from the past.*

IF MUSIC BE THE FOOD OF LOVE: HISTORIC FOODWAYS OF SALEM

They began now to gather in the small harvest they had…now began to come in store of fowl, as winter approached, of which this place did abound when they came first (but afterward decreased by degrees). And besides water fowl, there was great store of wild Turkeys, of which they took many, besides venison…Besides they had about a peck a meal a week to a person, or now since harvest, Indian corn. [Spelling modernized]
—*William Bradford's* History of Plimoth Plantation, *circa 1650*

Braving the awesome terrors of the sea, or rattling flesh and bones in a wagon across endless open country, many an immigrant has made that fearful journey with naught but a few material possessions or, perhaps, with nothing but hope and faith to make the unknown their home. But even if the newcomer arrives with a community of travelers, and with everything of a material nature needed to set up a household, two elements are truly needed to make any house, any town or any community truly feel like a haven.

Music—and Familiar Food

The music and the food of one's land of origin are essential to any gathering at which the concept of being home is central. Sanctuary without song and supper can hardly be imagined.

Music and food also provide gateways into understanding the ways others feel at home as well by helping to surmount barriers of language or appearance. This, too, builds community in a place of exile.

The sound of a beloved song from the past and the aroma of familiar food, soon to be set on the table—these treasures of human civilization make even the most difficult times seem somehow easier to bear and ensure that joyful times will be memorable and complete. Human beings have used food and music throughout history to furnish that feeling of well-being and security so essential to facing the future with courage and confidence.

Never is that more important than at times of celebration and holiday, especially in a country so rich in newcomers as the United States. Imported customs, music, and food eventually formed the new traditions of each holiday as immigrant groups settled in and wove their threads into the fabric of the community.

With this in mind, let's take a historical peek at some nineteenth-century New England winter holiday times.

During that century, when the United States truly began to define and embrace its own distinct identity, the legacies of many previously adopted new traditions were discernible and sometimes even self-consciously adopted as a way to reclaim so-called old-time American virtues.

To look fruitfully at Salem and local New England of the nineteenth century, however, first of all requires an understanding glance at the earliest European settlers on these rocky shores. Those mostly English immigrants brought with them a long, shared cultural heritage of secular music; it is good to remember that much of this music grew out of and honored the cycles and feasts of the natural and agricultural year.

As do most cultures of the world, the English colonists enjoyed frequent feasts of thanksgiving, particularly at the multiple harvest times of late summer and fall (e.g., Lammas Day, Harvest Home)—a tradition that our own Thanksgiving Day celebrations echo to this day, albeit now condensed to an official once-a-year holiday. Song always accompanied these celebrations.

The Puritan settlers, of course, also employed a natural—yet dogmatic and very carefully prescribed—expression of faith through song as prayer. It is highly significant that the first book printed in the New World was *The Whole Booke of Psalmes Faithfully Translated into English Metre*, commonly known as *The Bay Psalm Book*, which was printed in Massachusetts. The cultural legacy of this early book remained influential for more than one hundred years.

Consider one facet of that legacy: While designed to be affordable to most, which made individual participation in cultural activity accessible (not just in religious services, but as shared musical expression), it is also important to note that the authoritative nature of this book and other early guides solidified which texts and behavioral expressions were sanctioned. Deviance from this established norm became highly risky behavior that was easily discerned and chastised.

Colonists also brought with them deeply ingrained expectations, preferences, and prejudices in the matter of food. Those early Massachusetts colonists to this coast also shared a mostly middle-class background and a worldview shaped not only by their faith but by the inherited customs and techniques of English husbandry. Englishmen turned Puritan are still Englishmen, first and foremost.

Confronted with the wilderness of the new land, they set out to re-create the agricultural landscapes of their homeland, to tame the new land and institute the familiar foods of England no matter the challenge. This mindset,

Colonial Table
Setting, Pioneer
Village in Salem,
Massachusetts.
Courtesy of author.

more enduring in the New England colonies than other colonies of North America, shaped much of the development of a determined self-sufficiency and a marked tendency to insularity in New England's culture.

A Culinary Legacy

What were they used to? Colonists brought with them a medieval culinary heritage that relied heavily on seasonings in foods and a pronounced preference for meat, bread, and ale. The best bread was made from refined wheat flour and was white. The darker the bread, the less desirable; it was considered plebeian fare, so rye, oats, and barley represented settling for less. Beer was a favored drink and was enjoyed night and day. It was made from a wide variety of ingredients, but barley and hops were standard. Such plants and other herbs would grow in the all-important kitchen gardens of each homemaker.

They also enjoyed most fish and seafood. The new land proved hospitable in supplying them with abundance in this regard.

Native Americans not only gave examples of harvesting and preparing such bounty but taught other uses of fish in cultivation. The Europeans were also accustomed to making porridge from peas and beans and enjoyed cabbage and root vegetables like parsnips and carrots.

A long heritage of folkways attended the cultivation of beloved orchard fruits. Cider was consumed throughout the day. English settlers proudly transplanted a legacy of dairying, cheese and butter making to their new home as well.

As the observations of William Bradford, Salem's first minister, Francis Higginson, and others made clear, the land was beneficent indeed, and those back in England to whom they reported could scarcely believe the accounts of variety and abundance of food in the New World.

Whatever the fruitful potential of the land, however, most of the English settlers did not necessarily admire, nor did they wish to emulate, the migratory life led by the Native Americans, who followed the bounty of the seasons and moved their habitat accordingly. A moveable feast did not signify home to the Europeans; no, the settlement had to be permanent.

"When we came first to Nehum-kek, we found about half a score houses, and a faire house newly built for the Governor, we found also abboundance of corne planted by them, very good and well liking…We that are settled at Salem make what haste we can to build houses, so that within a short time we shall have a faire towne,[*sic*]" Higginson wrote in his *New-Englands Plantation* in 1630.[48]

Native Americans combined hunting, gathering and an agricultural system that centered on growing beans, squash (pumpkin) and maize (the Three Sisters) in a companion-planting arrangement that benefited the health of all three food staples. Although they did adopt such methods at first, such planting was unlike the furrowed rows of seedlings the English were familiar with and trusted. They preferred to plant seeds from overseas rather than utilize indigenous varieties.

Some dietary staples, however, continued elusive. Europeans missed having salt and sugar, but most of all they missed their best bread. The colonists would find, despite their hunger to re-create the English farm and foods, the resistance of the land to some of their desires—especially in the matter of growing wheat—compelled them to adopt some native foods.

One can hardly overestimate the importance, in this regard, of corn. It was the adoption of Indian maize into European food that would affect the establishment of a truly American way of cooking, lead to the first American cookbook and ironically engender some of the first traditional New England foods. Receipts, or recipes, for the common English meal of pudding, using Indian corn achieved the marriage of Old and New Worlds in a tangible and edible way.

Later generations of New Englanders would hark back to these foods made with corn when, in the face of rapidly changing demographics due to sustained and increased immigration, they would try to self-consciously reclaim the "good solid food of our grandmothers" as an assertion of cultural continuity.

To this theme, we shall return.

Some Salem Feasts and Festivities, Nineteenth-Century Style

Gentle Reader, take my hand and let's take a jaunt around town this winter eve in nineteenth-century Salem. Ladies, be sure to take your shawls of Indian cashmere, and you might wear your chinchilla cap or pumpkin hood.

Gentlemen, perhaps you might kindly help us into a sleigh as it goes collecting us door to door this cold winter evening and then jump in yourselves. We're bound for peek into some Salem homes and then we'll be headed for a night of music, dancing and, of course, a festive shared supper.

Hearken to the musical sounds of a joyous Salem, feasting and making merry in winter holidays past. The melodic voices of the past echo still. Since imagination laughs at boundaries, and we are but silent observers of these scenes, we'll wander at will between the years.

> *Thanksgiving Ball.*
>
> *MR. MAURICE most respectfully informs the LADIES & GENTLEMEN OF SALEM, and its vicinity, that his BALL will be on THANKSGIVING EVENING, (Thursday next) when he will be supremely happy to wait on them.*
>
> *TICKETS may be had of HIM, at Mrs. BALDWIN's and at Mr. CARLTON's Printing-Office*
> —*The* Salem Imperial Register, *November 24, 1800*

Music, music, music...

> *Mr. HOLYOKE, President of the Essex Musical Society, has just published some ORIGINAL MUSIC, suitable for Thanksgiving. It consists of an*

ANTHEM, a LYRIC POEM, and a DOXOLOGY; composed in a familiar style. They may be had by dozen, or single one, of CUSHING & APPLETON.
—*The* Salem Gazette, *Friday, September 17, 1802*

Shall we dance (and eat)?

In 1859 the Salem Assemblies were revived at Hamilton Hall, with a modest simplicity suited to the short reign of economy following in the wake of '57. At the close of the season a "Lady's Ball" was given, on which occasion Mr. John Remond, the ancient caterer of 1805, sent a large glass bowl used at the parties of that remote period, asking to have it placed on the supper table… The first assembly took place the Thursday after Christmas, in 1805.

Everything was order and decorum, from the managers down to the waiting-maids. The numbers were called at half past six; supper at ten; music dismissed at twelve.

Mrs. Remond, the wife of the caterer, will be remembered for her charming manners and good cooking. Her mock-turtle soup, venison or alamode beef, and roast chickens, with perhaps ducks, and light, not flaky pastry, made an ample feast for a dozen gentlemen at the fashionable hour of two o'clock. Dinners then had one advantage over dinners now,—the guests knew what they were eating.

> *The courtly minuet*
> *And long-lined country dance*
> *(For beaux and belles as yet*
> *Had no quadrilles from France)*
> *Were seen upon the floor.*
> *As the dancers swam or flew,*
> *With graces hovering o'er,*
> *When this old bowl was new.*

—*Marianne Cabot (Devereux) Silsbee,* A Half Century in Salem, *1887*

Come to tea and bring your appetite.

The richer style of cooking was chiefly used on festive occasions…At that early date we still used the ponderous methods which had come down to us from our English ancestors, and the lighter, more wholesome French treatment of materials was not known.

Salem was more famous in those early days for its delightful and cosy tea parties than for any great literary interests…as everybody had dined in the middle of the day, the guests brought good appetites to the feast...silver tea-pots for both green and black tea and the coffee or chocolate pot...sugar bowl, cream pitcher and slop bowl belonging to the tea service.

It was the custom of the day to cool your tea before drinking it by pouring it into your saucer...cooked oysters, and chickens or game dressed in different ways...a noble chicken pie...silver cake baskets with pound, sponge, and fruit cake...different kinds of bread and hot cakes, olives, tongue, and ham cut after Judge Story's formula, who used to say that the only proper way to serve ham was to cut it so thin that one could see to read a newspaper between the slices...preserves, whole quinces floating in their rich clear juice being always present and damsons and preserved ginger. Does this sound messy and horrid?

—*Caroline Howard King,* When I Lived in Salem, 1822–1866

Oh, my aching stomach, and—er, yeah—that other stuff, too.

DYSPEPSIA, OR...INDIGESTION

THIS prevalent disorder, as it exhibits itself in its customary symptoms of want of appetite, distressing flatulencies, heartburn, pain in the stomach, sick headache, nausea, vomiting, and restiveness, is now found to yield to the tried efficacy of DR RELFE'S VEGETABLE SPECIFIC, AND ANTI BILIOUS PILLS.

These two preparations combined...an efficacious remedy for the Dyspepsia even after it has acquired the most obstinate character and resisted every effort of professional skill...Price 50 cents each box. For sale at retail, for public convenience, at the Druggists generally, in Salem and Vicinity, viz.

James R. Buffam
Whipple & Lawrence
J.D. Chandler
E. Porter...(Salem)
A large discount made to dealers.

—*Advertisement,* Salem Gazette, October 21, 1828

BROWN OR DYSPEPSIA BREAD—This bread is now best known as "Graham bread"—not that Doctor Graham invented or discovered the manner of its preparation, but that he has been unwearied and successful in recommending it to the public. It is an excellent article of diet for the

dyspeptic and the costive, and for most persons of sedentary habits, would be beneficial.
—Sarah Josepha Hale, Early American Cookery: The Good Housekeeper, *1841*

More of us may have wanted to celebrate Christmas, but…

[Thanksgiving] *was a happy time, and it was happily kept…Old family jokes were laughed over, healths were drunk and toasts given, old songs sung…In the evening games were played and there were music and dances and charades…*Auld Lang Syne *being sometimes sung before parting for the night.*

There was no observance of Christmas in those days in Salem…There was still too strong a Puritan element in New England to admit of a celebration of the chief festival of the Episcopal Church, so we rather inconsistently substituted the pagan New Year…in our family, we had a small celebration on Christmas Eve, when my father always read to us the Christmas Canto in Marmion, and Milton's Hymn of the Nativity.
—Caroline Howard King, When I Lived in Salem, *1822-1866*

And some of us always *had* celebrated Christmas:

New Musick.

Just published, and ready for sale…The American Harmony *containing a select number of Odes, Anthems, and plain Tunes, composed for performance on Thanksgivings, Ordinations, Christmas, Fasts, Funeral and other occasions: The whole entirely new:—By Oliver Holden—Teacher of Musick, in Charlestown.*

Books may be had of W. Carleton, the Bible and Heart, Salem.
Subscribers are requested to call for their Books.
Charlestown, Oct. 10, 1792
—Advertisement, Salem Gazette, *October 23, 1792*

Puddings, made from a variety of foodstuffs, were most often bag boiled and were not always sweet. Interestingly, Federalist Salemites ate their puddings as the first course or early in the meal; Jeffersonian Democrats ate theirs as the last course.

Hmmm. Puddings as the decisive word in political contests: now there's a concept!

After the Civil War, American society underwent accelerated change. An enlarging middle- and upper-class structure based on economic success (albeit success subject to cycles of panic or recession) characterized the era.

Industrialization and commerce boomed, particularly in the North. For Salem, though the town was slower to industrialize, commerce no longer meant exclusively maritime adventures.

Throughout the land, a flood of immigration resumed and intensified, which, of course, saw an expansion of ethnic groups already well represented in the established American populace. However, quite significantly, the post-bellum years also saw a new tide of non-English-speaking and more religiously diverse peoples.

Urban centers diffused into newly developed suburbs, and those who achieved a middle-class and higher economic status began to seek the amenities such transfers bestowed. This included an increased specialization of rooms within a home; by midcentury the growing importance of a separate space for tasteful, civil, and socialized dining experiences was evident in all accounts—informal, private or public—made by many observers of the conventions of the day.

The effect of the multiple and rapid changes in society led to an interesting mélange: the conscious adoption of the new and modern and abrogation of certain restraints as the full-blown pursuit of wealth preoccupied post-bellum America. Yet palpable anxiety surfaced as social status fluctuated along with a nagging sense of moral decay.

How to deal with this social anxiety? Well, many of those coping mechanisms won't surprise you. How you dressed, where you lived, what kind of occupation you had or didn't have—these are all familiar ways of establishing or maintaining a social identity. Despite Thoreau's dictum not to trust enterprises that require new clothes, many a person anxious about their social standing did just that, no matter what era you examine, and the nineteenth century was replete with authoritative guides on just what to wear, when and where to wear it and how to wear it.

Such books also touted the desirability of musical activity in the home as a mark of gentility and culture, and the conduct of the informal, after-dinner musical evening was also carefully outlined.

> 2581. *If you can sing or play, do so at once when requested, without requiring to be pressed, or make a fuss.*
> 2582. *On the other hand, let your performance be brief, or, if ever so good, it will be tiresome.*

2583. When a lady sits down to the pianoforte, some gentleman should attend her, arrange the music-stool, and turn over the leaves.

2584. Do not make yourself too conspicuous in those attentions.

2616. Never converse while a person is singing; it is an insult not only to the singer, but to the company.

2617. The essential part of good breeding is the practical desire to afford pleasure, and to avoid giving pain. Any man possessing this desire, requires only opportunity and observation to make him a gentleman.

—*Sarah Josepha Hale,* Mrs. Hale's Receipts For The Million: Containing Four Thousand Five Hundred And Forty-Five Receipts, Facts, Directions, Etc. In The Useful, Ornamental, And Domestic Arts, And In The Conduct Of Life, *1857*

If one followed all these guides religiously, the results not only indicated your class and good breeding but were also as indicative of a worldview as surely as singing tunes from the *Bay Psalm Book* did in colonial days.

It might surprise you to realize that what you ate, Gentle Reader, also mattered a great deal in this arena; where you ate it, who prepared it and how you presented it were hallmarks of social identity, too.

Countless guides for the American housekeeper (always female, often accompanied by other females—the much-discussed "help") present the kitchen and dining table as the altars of exhibiting respectability and virtue.

Excess was deplored as indicative of moral laxity. These books and magazine articles were often couched in language worthy of any Sunday-morning preacher.

Even the food-related furniture reflected this. Late nineteenth-century sideboards in dining rooms became elaborate icons of culinary domesticity, echoing, in appearance, actual church altars.

And, by the turn of the century, the music you enjoyed—or, more to the point, publicly patronized—also became absorbed into these prescriptive social-identity mechanisms. For the new American, for the upwardly mobile, here were guides to achieving integration.

However, these two areas of life—food and music—also grew into some of the most obvious tools "old stock" Americans utilized to declare and emphasize their social identity in the face of changing demographics. The reactive dissonance of stressing good, old American virtues to the new immigrants in a modern democracy is particularly noteworthy to a historian.

What is fascinating here is that preparing and eating certain traditional foods, in the context of a revival of an idealized Old New England, became somewhat of a fetish. It is almost amusing to note the preponderance of nineteenth-century receipts that utilized those humble colonial adoptions of Native American foods, dishes such as those that used cornmeal, pumpkin, and beans.

Other dishes designated as sober and solid old-time American food were baked apples, meat potpies and puddings, chowder, hoecake or johnnycake, pandowdy, doughnuts and, in general, usage of molasses in a variety of ways.

Cooking these dishes, some once denigrated as foreign, now became emblematic of the struggle by some against distressing change. Of course, these meals originated in a time when colonists adopted Native American foods as mere stopgaps on the way to replicating traditional English farms and culture in the New World. But clinging to them in the nineteenth century became a hallmark of old-school values for these folk.

We could explore the nooks and crannies of this phenomenon endlessly. And I haven't even touched on the adoption of French cooking as a marker of class and status.

However, I'll end this discussion with a quick glance at a parlor we visited last time. Since coffee and tea were so central to the rituals of socialized dining—and nearly everyone, including children, drank these beverages—it seems fitting to drop you off at a Salem tea party.

Remember Caroline King's "cosy tea parties" where "it was the custom of the day to cool your tea before drinking it by pouring it into your saucer"?

This custom, which originated in China, was considered old fashioned by the middle of the nineteenth century. The Chinese method employed the teacup for brewing the leaves and the dish was used as a lid while the tea brewed. When finished, the tea was then rather naturally poured into the dish for drinking—hence the references found throughout memoirs and literature to "a dish of tea."

Perhaps unsurprisingly, in Salem, with its strong material, emotional, and historical ties to the overseas trade, the custom continued to charm long after sufficient chiding by etiquette books that labeled the practice inappropriate to those who wished to be considered sophisticated. Judging by the mass production of cup plates in the mid-nineteenth century, however, it would seem that this once-exotic and now old-school custom persisted in the popular taste well beyond the borders of this city renamed for peace, remaining in everyday use to the end of the century.

The cook I had for my sweetheart,
I'll tell you the reason why,

At Christmas times she baked plum pudding,
And likewise made mince pie;
She said in the cupboard she had good store
And she did keep the keys,
One pocket I should fill with butter,
And the other should fill with cheese,
And the other should fill with cheese.
—*From a song in broadside form;* The Cook I Had for My Sweet Heart

Receipts

Let's leave you with some hands-on experiences.

In researching this material, I garnered strange looks from my long-suffering husband as I muttered to myself while studying some of the earliest American cookbooks. Strange–because I am not known for my culinary prowess. In fact, in family lore, I am known as the "girl who fried water," dropped a cake and watched it skitter across the floor like a solid-wood hockey puck before shattering. I victimized all comers with similar kitchen misadventures.

But devotion to history made me brave.

So here are three tried-out-and-eaten, yet-we-survived-'em dishes you can make, too, that have been drawn from ancient and sundry cookbooks. Let me know how they work for you!

A Nice Indian Pudding, from Amelia Simmons's *American Cookery,* 1796:
"No. 2. 3 pints scalded milk to one pint meal salted; cool, add 2 eggs, 4 ounces butter, sugar or molasses and spice q. f. it will require two and half hours baking."

Modern folks: Preheat oven to 275 degrees Fahrenheit, or 135 degrees Celsius, and lightly grease a nine-by-nine-inch baking dish.

We stirred 1/2 cup yellow cornmeal slowly into the scalded milk, placed in a double boiler. We used less butter, and 1 egg. We then put in 2/3 cup blackstrap molasses, 1 teaspoon salt; mixed it all together; poured it into the baking dish, and stirred 2 cups cold milk into that mixture. We baked it for about 3 hours. (If I was to make this again, I would lighten up on the molasses a bit.)

This makes a dark, sweet, very dense pudding. Serve with some whipped cream and try not to count any calories!

Blancmange, Dyspepsia and All That—The Real Thing!

One night over dinner (which was cooked by a real chef—in a restaurant) I fretted over additional recipes to share with you from our little collection of historical cookbooks.

One decision I already had made: to try dyspepsia bread, since wailing about this ubiquitous ailment was such a continuous activity throughout the nineteenth century. It was no wonder: the lengthy menus for most New England feasts, plus the copious use of butter, sugar (molasses), salt, and heavy meats give me indigestion just reading them!

The other? Well, just as many girls do, ever since reading *Little Women* as a child, I have wondered how blancmange would taste. And, of course, in that book the character that made it "very nicely"—Meg—shares my own name. Good karma there, I hoped.

What wasn't so nice was my completely befuddled self wandering in the grocery baking supplies aisle exploring what was, for me, as exotic a land as the icy tundra is to a hula dancer. My Jim finally had to rescue me from my frozen—frozen as in deer-in-the-headlights—contemplation of the endless stretches of flours, mixes, spices and gadgets the use of which—well, I frankly have no earthly clue as to their use.

But I made these recipes and, once again, lived to tell you about them. Enjoy! And if you make them, too, please let me know how it worked out.

Dyspepsia bread from Lydia M. Child's *The American Frugal Housewife*, 1841:

"*The American Farmer* publishes the following receipt for making bread, which has proved highly salutary to persons afflicted with that complaint, viz: —Three quarts unbolted wheat meal; one quart soft water, warm, but not hot; one gill of fresh yeast; one gill of molasses, or not, as may suit the taste; one tea-spoonful of saleratus.

"This will make two loaves, and should remain in the oven at least one hour; and when taken out, placed where they will cool gradually. Dyspepsia crackers can be made with unbolted flour, water and saleratus."

Modern cooks: A gill is 8 large tablespoonfuls. We simply used a premeasured 1/4 ounce package of yeast. Saleratus is baking soda. Baked for one hour in a 400-degree oven. It comes out dense, dark, bland, crusty.

Blancmange from Sarah Josepha Hale's "Early American Cookery" in *The Good Housekeeper*, 1841:

Maggi's first blancmange. It was even edible. *Courtesy of author.*

This is used as the backdrop for the modern Salem History Society logo. *Courtesy of author.*

"Rice blancmange: Simmer a teacupful of whole rice in the least water possible, till it almost bursts, then add half a pint of good milk or thin cream, and boil it until it is quite a mash, stirring it the whole time it is on the fire, that it may not burn. Dip a mould in cold water, and pour the hot rice in and let it stand till cold, when it will come easily out.

"This dish may be eaten with cream and sugar, or custard and preserved fruits; raspberries are best. It should be made the day before it is wanted.

"It can be flavored with spices, lemon-peel, & etc., and sweetened with a little loaf sugar; it is then very excellent."

The proof of my success here, Gentle Reader, was in the tastiness of my first blancmange, a photo of which I share with you.

"CÉAD MILE FAILTE": THE GREEN FIELDS OF AMERICA (IRISH IN SALEM)

On March 17, 1787, a year in which human freedom and dignity were celebrated by the drafting of the Constitution of the United States, there was an unusual notice was reprinted in a Salem, Massachusetts newspaper.

Under the banner, "EUROPE: IRELAND," which was dated "Dublin, Oct. 24," the *Salem Mercury: Political, Commercial, and Moral*'s reprint offered a provocative alternative view of the causes of "ignorance of the Irish peasantry." An alternative, that is, to the usual practice of ascribing the immigrants' deficits to the practice of their fiercely-maligned Catholic religion.

> *Oppression, the very parent of ignorance...The penal statutes, in the unalterable nature of things, must have made the wretches poor—& yet they are upbraided with poverty...they starve...[there is] a mere want of employment—and yet they are branded with the ephitet, idle. It would not be more absurd, to put out a man's eyes, & then censure him for not seeing, than to reproach the wretched Irish with their present state.*

Perhaps, the *Mercury*'s broadminded outlook owed some debt to the influence of Benjamin Franklin, who upon visiting Dublin drew sharp distinctions between England and Ireland in 1771. Some signers of the Declaration of Independence and of the Constitution were of Irish descent, and the Irish served honorably in the Revolutionary War (as Bostonians remember when they celebrate Evacuation Day, aka St. Patrick's Day).

"A Celtic Cross." Original drawing by author.

Yet, a notice so sympathetic to the Irish Catholic in an early New England newspaper is worthy of some attention.

The Penal Statutes were enacted by the Ireland's Protestant English government in 1695. Worse than previous edicts, they were intended to erase Irish Catholic civil rights, to control matters of dress, language and laws. As an effective strategy, the codes required an oath of abjuration of the Catholic religion for those who wished to retain even nominal citizenship.

Irish Catholics were forbidden to become teachers and denied access to education; clergy were expelled; Catholic burial was prohibited; and property was forfeited.

The Popery act of 1704 and similar ones that followed intensified the oppression to an almost unimaginable pitch. Roman Catholics were forbidden to purchase or inherit land, vote, become lawyers, or marry Protestants. Irish industries were suppressed.

This program of dispossession and disenfranchisement created intolerable conditions in Ireland, filling the country with starving and homeless refugees. It compelled massive immigration to the North American colonies, which swelled during the famine years.

Yet, once in the New World, the bitterness of forced and desperate exile was often compounded by encountering deep-seated and enduring prejudice and discriminatory attitudes that continued to threaten survival—even in the Land of the Free.

Outside of enclaves founded en masse by immigrants (e.g., Londonderry, New Hampshire) or the somewhat more hospitable shores of Southern states (e.g., Maryland), those with the wherewithal or skills were able, once they landed, to move on and up.

One group, however, could not move on—those who arrived penniless, unskilled, unhealthy, unconnected.

Oscar Handlin's classic work *Boston's Immigrants* describes the problematic situation that ensued. "Only one country directed a dislodged population to a city where no promise dwelled; elsewhere events promoted the departure of those only who could choose their destination more prudently." A "startled" Boston and environs faced the flood.

The problem became more acute after the Irish poor law, which "integrated emigration and eviction into a new economic policy," was enacted in 1838 and further compounded by the famine years.

Most early Irish Catholic immigrants in eighteenth-century Massachusetts would indeed find the road rocky and the climb desperately difficult.

Irish ways and customs were repulsed as alien. Legacies from oppression, forbidden education and forced displacement would hinder progress.

Anti-Irish discrimination in the United States would continue well into the next century.

Yet, by end of the nineteenth century, the Irish American story becomes one of hope, courage and success.

Some of those happy stories I will address later. But to wrap up now, let's take just a tiny historical peek at how Salem marked Ireland's most enduring transplant.

St. Patrick's Day (Lá 'le Pádraig)

Celtic sacred days begin at sundown the evening before the named day.

Originally, in Ireland, as here, St. Patrick's feast day was celebrated as a religious holiday and a temporary reprieve from the privation of Lenten fasting.

Folk observances included *not* the wearing of shamrocks but the making of St. Patrick's Crosses by children and adults and drinking the *Pota Pádraig*, or St. Patrick's pot.

Into the final glass of this festive beverage was thrown a shamrock, a plant of ancient Triadic symbolism that was adopted by Christianity and Ireland as a symbol of the Trinity and of the nation, respectively. After thus "drowning the shamrock," the plant was thrown over the left shoulder. These customs had folk and ritual significance.

The later development of widespread "wearing of green," of shamrocks and secular parties and proud nationalistic parades would become part of the great success story that is nineteenth- and twentieth-century Irish American history.

Witness those stirrings here:

Salem Gazette, *March 19, 1880. "A quiet St. Patrick's...The first pleasant St. Patrick's Day in seven years, on Wednesday."*

Salem Evening News, *March 17, 1900. "IN ENGLAND. St. Patrick's Day is Celebrated—FOR THE FIRST TIME—in the History of Great Britain; All Wear Green. London. March 17. For the first time in history St. Patrick's Day was generally observed in England. The green flag was hoisted over Windsor castle."*

Salem Evening News, March 17, 1900. "SHAMROCKS—The Boutonniere in Style Today—ST. PATRICK'S DAY—Observed at Catholic Churches; Other Celebrations…Not many years ago it was the custom of the local organizations of men of Irish blood to observe the feast with public demonstrations…but…for years has not been observed in Salem…The only local observance of the feast will be held by Essex court of Foresters… Several persons were seen wearing shamrocks or other green favors."

Salem Evening News, March 18, 1910. "IRELAND'S GREAT SAINT HONORED BY SALEMITES—Several Societies Held Banquets and Exercises in Honor of St. Patrick Last Night; Green Was Quite Prominent About City Yesterday."

Beannachtaí na Féile Pádraig agaibh!
Blessings of the Feast of Patrick To You!

St. Mary's–Immaculate Conception Parish, as it is today. The original St. Mary's Church, 1820, was "the first Catholic church dedicated to Mary in New England. In 1826, led by Father John Mahoney of Ireland, it became the first Catholic parish outside of Boston." *Courtesy of author.*

"Farewell to the Groves of Shillelagh and Shamrock…As Far Away o'er the Ocean I am Bound."

In the Old Irish (Gaelic) language, the only word for leaving home is *deorai*, or exile.

And yet, from the 1600s on, both Protestant and Catholic Irish took that terrible soul-wrenching step. In the seventeenth century, more than 100,000 Irish—the largest proportion of them young, single men—left their homeland for what was referred to in song after song as "the green fields of America."

Some went to Canada. Others in this early migration tended to settle from Pennsylvania to Georgia and many would move west. This group of Irish immigrants was largely of Scotch–Irish descent and typically Presbyterian.

Irish Catholics also immigrated to American shores early and often, but the major Catholic diaspora would roll over the sea during the nineteenth century. The catastrophic effects of the British government's programs for eradication of Irish culture, industry, employment, and society were compounded by blight-induced failure of the potato crops. Potatoes were the only food remaining for Irish sustenance after paying taxes and rent. The suffering that resulted defies comprehension.

The Great Irish Starvation of the 1840s compelled five million Irish people to embrace a desperate exile. They took with them searing memories of a lost homeland; many harbored bitterness against the English for their loss. Most felt a fierce determination to rectify displacement. All of this would play a decisive role in the trajectory of Irish American history.

The Irish who immigrated in such a manner often disembarked in ports of entry like New York City, which had a history of absorbing them—the first St. Patrick's Day parade was held there in the 1760s—or in Boston, which did not. Anti-Catholicism was a virulent strain in New England as a whole and Massachusetts in particular.

According to Richard D. Brown and Jack Tager's *Massachusetts, a Concise History*, "Catholics could not worship publicly in Massachusetts until 1780… By 1820, an amended state constitutions allowed Catholics to hold office, but only Protestants could be school teachers."[49]

The entrepreneurial imperatives of the Industrial Revolution, and the challenges new immigrants brought to economic and social stasis (not to mention traditional sociopolitical dominance), compounded Yankee fears and religious enmity.

As for the immigrant, to see employment labeled "No Irish Need Apply" and being crowded into noisome tenement slums, bereft of religion, family and friends, was no joke. Immigrants hoping for a future with a job and a decent place to live and worship faced new horrors of injustice, disease, and social obstacles.

Situations became completely horrific with the rise of nativist movements such as the so-called Know-Nothing political party in antebellum America. By the mid-nineteenth century, neighborhoods and towns would sometimes become literal battlegrounds, conflagrations of unimaginable intensity.

Yet out of this, like the phoenix, the Irish would rise and forge political, social and economic success. The ability to vote was a precious component of this process. The proud constitutional legacy of vouchsafing civil rights prevailed, albeit not very smoothly.

The cultural importance of Irish song and story would also build and maintain ethnic identity and pride in exile even as ways of assimilation to the new homeland were achieved.

Shamrocks in Salem

According to local historian John Frayler's research, which my own studies to date have supported, "Salem's immigrant population was not exceptionally visible until about 1830. The most visible aspect of its existence was the presence of Catholics...In 1836...some 150–200 persons were noted as Catholic.

"Greater numbers of Irish began arriving about 1846...These people found employment at the newly built Naumkeag mills...and railroad construction primarily, with various general laborer and domestic occupations also represented."

Frayler's examination of birth records indicated that Salem's demographics had changed dramatically between 1908 and 1910. About $1/_3$, in his estimation, were "old Yankee or assimilated Irish, another $1/_3$ was French-Canadian...As late as 1953 Salem was listed as $1/_3$ Irish descent, $1/_3$ French-Canadian and of the remaining $1/_3$, the largest segment was Polish."[50]

Although Salem wasn't particularly welcoming to immigrants—Nathaniel Hawthorne, for instance, merely gave voice to common attitudes when he spoke of the drunken, "lazy" and "wild Irish" in his *Sketches from Memory* and *American Notebooks*—the Irish immigrants who settled here helped build, transform and revitalize the city.

Green Fields of America

Immigrants of any era or ethnicity have often found "green fields in America" in the entertainment business. But, more than most, the Irish in America have confirmed pride in ancient ethnic heritage, voiced a love of their new homeland and articulated the common hopes of humanity through the creative and performing arts.

Just as the offerings from the stage are shaped by audience expectations so, too, are the performers who change those expectations. So, with song and story, I will leave you. Each of these historical performances highlights a different facet of the emerald. Come and meet some of the Irish who came to Salem to entertain and to enlighten—to change and be changed.

1818—CONCERT of Vocal and Instrumental Music...at CONCERT HALL...Among the selections: Song—Exile of Erin

1891—Grand Gaelic Musical Festival AT Cadet Armory Hall, Salem.

1896—ONE NIGHT ONLY...The Prince of Romantic Actors, Mr. JAMES O'NEILL...in...Monte Cristo As played by Mr. O'Neill over 3000 times in all the leading theatres of United States and Canada.

1896—FAREWELL. Touching Scene at St. Mary's Hall. Fr. Hally's Parishioners Said Good-Bye. Men, as Well as Women, Gave Way to Tears. Retiring Pastor Presented with $1000 Check...A programme... was rendered. [Note: a great many (local) Irish performers listed]

1896—Donnelly & Girard in their Farcical Success, "THE RAINMAKERS"—Conroy and Fox...The Kings of Celtic Comedy...In... "O'Flarity's Vacation"—Cissy Fitzgerald in "The Foundling" [Note: known as "The Girl With the Wink"]

1901—THE FAVORITE FUN MAKERS—FERGUSON AND MACK...In... McCarthy's Mishaps...ALL NEW FUN.

1902—ETHEL BARRYMORE IN Capt. Jinks of the Horse Marines...A Fantastic Comedy, in Three Acts. [Note: Ethel's uncle, John Drew, would play Salem in 1912. His father was born in Dublin.]

1902—ANDREW MACK, In His Greatest Success TOM MOORE…During the action of the play, Mr. Mack will introduce Thomas Moore's "Evelyn's Bower," "Love's Young Dream," "The Last Rose of Summer." [Note: Mack, who acted in many Irish plays, won praise for his fine tenor voice.]

1905—Walter C. Kelly—The Greatest of All Monologue Artists and Story Tellers. [Note: Walter C. Kelly was a long-lasting headliner and uncle of film actress Grace Kelly.]

1908—EMPIRE THEATRE—John L. Sullivan. [Note: Boxing legend Sullivan, born in Roxbury, appeared in vaudeville after retiring from the ring in 1894.]

1908—HIS HONOR THE MAYOR with Harry Kelly…same production as…New York, Boston, and Chicago.

1908—MR. DANIEL RYAN…In a High Class Repertoire…THE BELLS.

1908—LOUISE VALE…In the Charming Romantic Play…The Girl of the Emerald Isle.

1911—ENGAGEMENT EXTRAORDINARY—IRISH PLAYERS—From the Irish National Theatre, Dublin. [Note: this engagement *was* extraordinary, with plays by W.B. Yeats, William Boyle and Lady Gregory.]

At long last, the Irish Renaissance had come to Salem.

SUBSTANCE AND SHADOW: PHOTOGRAPHY AT THE PEM

My greatest aim has been to advance the art of photography and to make it what I think I have, a great and truthful medium of history.
—Mathew B. Brady (1822–1896)

"A photograph is a secret about a secret. The more it tells you the less you know.
—Diane Arbus (1923–1971)

It began as a bridge of light and time.

At the University of Texas at Austin, "housed in its original presentational frame and sealed within an atmosphere of inert gas in an airtight steel and plexiglas storage frame," lies a unique, one-of-a-kind object that "must be viewed under controlled lighting in order for its image to be visible…within a darkened environment free of other incidental light sources."[51]

In the summer of 1826, Joseph Nicéphore Niépce (1765–1833) set up a camera obscura at an upper-story window at his country house, Le Gras, in Saint-Loup-de-Varennes. After a daylong exposure, it produced the first permanent photograph from nature.

The heliograph, as Niépce called it, showed the upper loft of his family's house, a pear tree lacing the sky, a long, slanting barn roof and the chimney of a bake house. On the other side of the photograph, an additional wing of the main house could be seen. Even after eight hours, the photograph was underexposed, making the finished scene faint and difficult to see.

Remarkably, due to the lengthy process, this first photograph shows, simultaneously, the shadows of both morning and afternoon. The arc of a full day has been captured and merged in one image.

This photograph is a historical bridge; past and present of a sun's daily arc through the open sky are intertwined and etched forever, captured in light and shadow.

Where the Past and the Present Meet

The sky itself seems to soar through the sunlit atrium at Salem's Peabody Essex Museum (PEM), where "presenting art and culture in new ways… linking past and present…embracing artistic and cultural achievements worldwide" is an ongoing mission, according to the museum's website.

With roots extending to 1799 when the founding of the East India Marine Society celebrated the thriving maritime economy of Salem's early years, the museum can be seen as a bridge between historical worlds and distant shores.

Founded by Salem captains and entrepreneurs cresting the waves of Salem's worldwide trade, the early East India Marine Society collected from its members objects of the northwest coast of America, Africa, Asia, Oceania, the East Indies and India and housed them in a so-called "cabinet of natural and artificial curiosities." So, as was the toast by a seaman in 1804, "that every mariner may possess the history of the world."[52]

East India Marine Hall. *From C.H. Webber and Winfield S. Nevins's* Old Naumkeag: An Historical Sketch of the City of Salem, and the Towns of Marblehead, Peabody, Beverly, Danvers, Wenham, Manchester, Topsfield, and Middleton.

At the PEM's Phillips Library in four rooms with rows of filing cabinets and shelves of boxes, an immense collection of images stands silent witness to these years of world exploration.

"These are the maritime images alone," photo archives and resources manager Christine Michelini told me as we walked into one of those rooms in 2009. They line an entire wall in the archive.

Enthusiastically, she pointed out historical photographs of sea-grizzled Swampscott fishermen seated stoically dockside, gazing expressionlessly at the camera. Another drawer holds images of every kind of ship imaginable, from multiple eras and in myriad formats: photographic, etched, and drawn.

She gently pulled exquisite glass lantern slides from a drawer in a crowded back room and held up to the light the colors of India and Asia that gleam, jewel-like, in the hand. These are truly marvels to behold.

A particular point of pride for the PEM and for Michelini is the museum's online image resource, the Essex Image Vault (http://esseximages.com), which has, as she says, "striking images of the past" that especially appealed to her and the photo archive team as images "people would be interested in." It represents a valuable online resource for those eager for an accessible visual window into aspects of Essex County's history.

Through a Modern Lens

In an upper-floor gallery at the PEM, a new exhibit made waves of a different kind.

Lining walls the color of an old-fashioned maroon theater curtain and washed in quiet, soft light hung a landscape of surf, sky, human bodies and beautiful boards. The installation represented the inaugural exhibit by newly appointed curator of photography Phillip Prodger and marked the launch of a new photography department at the museum.

An acclaimed author and art historian, Prodger would seem to be the perfect curator for the PEM's new department. He holds a PhD in art history from Cambridge University and attended Williams College and Stanford University.

A scholar who displayed the intelligence and charm of the consummate gentleman during our interviews, he is the author of *Darwin's Camera: Art and Photography in the Theory of Evolution* (Oxford University Press, (2009), which has been described as "the extraordinary story of how Charles Darwin changed the way pictures are seen and made."

An article in the journal *Leonardo* by Amy Ione described Prodger's curatorial gifts for the exhibit "Time Stands Still: Muybridge and the Instantaneous Photography Movement": "Rather than interpreting the Stanford and Muybridge collaboration, guest curator Philip Prodger places their joint legacy within a larger context relying on roughly 170 works, culled from collections in six countries."[53]

This bodes well for future museum experiences representing not only the contemporary art for which the PEM is known, but its deep historic roots in Salem by honoring its existing collection of superlative and historically significant photography.

As importantly, it will also highlight those aspects of fun and enjoyment that photography, the most democratic of art forms, so aptly presents.

Prodger's first curated exhibit, "Surfland," underscored this observation. Here one found contemporary images by photographer Joni Sternbach, modern tintypes produced by using a nineteenth-century technique, and poignant archival tintypes and daguerreotypes concurrently displayed.

The tintype, also known as a ferrotype, was introduced in the mid-nineteenth century. It is produced on metallic sheet—not tin—by a wet plate process; the images recorded are reversed, as in a mirror. It was, for its time, relatively inexpensive, thus popular among average people. Tintypes produced a rugged and durable photograph that could be mailed or carried (which was common during the Civil War).

This excerpt from a nineteenth-century photographic chemistry manual may serve to illustrate some of what Sternbach experienced in shooting her subjects live on the beach:

> *The Collodion process may be applied with success to landscape Photography; but as the plates become dry and lose their sensitiveness shortly after their removal from the Bath, the operator will require to provide himself with a yellow tent or some portable vehicle in which the operations of sensitizing and developing can be conducted. As it is a point of great importance in the Collodion process that the plate should receive exactly the right amount of exposure in the Camera,—a few seconds more or less sufficing to affect the character of the picture,—many will submit to much trouble and inconvenience in order to have the apparatus complete upon the spot at which the view is taken.*[54]

Needless to say, you get to know your subjects with this technique a bit better than taking a digital snapshot; that became a functional part of the process for Sternbach. Perhaps this lent a sympathetic undertone to the otherwise anthropological aspect of these photographs.

Bridging the Past and the Future

In later life, the great nineteenth-century American icon of human rights advocacy Sojourner Truth (circa 1797–1883) supported herself by selling her photographic portraits as cabinet cards and carte-de-visites. Many bore her quoted words: "I sell the Shadow to support the Substance."

The photographer Ansel Adams (1902–1984) pointed out that "a photograph is usually looked at—seldom looked into."

A photograph, unlike a painting, seems perhaps so familiar and so domestic that we forget that we are gazing only at chemically captured bits of light and dark, substance and shadow. A photograph, however contemporary it may seem, is inherently and inescapably historical. It has only captured a second of time past.

Frenchman Joseph Nicéphore Niépce had, both figuratively and literally, captured time in substance and shadow. Photography continues to bestow this gift on those of us who regularly walk the bridges linking past, present and future.

Photographs are mirrors we aim at ourselves.

Think of this next time you aim your little digital box of light and shadow at the world.

Chapter 3

Legacy Locations

"INCALCULABLE ADVANTAGES"
—SALEM'S PUBLIC LIBRARY

In the spring of 1731, disappointed...

Chapter 3

Legacy Locations

"INCALCULABLE ADVANTAGES"
—SALEM'S PUBLIC LIBRARY

In the spring of 1731, disappointed with the result of a private sharing library experiment, Benjamin Franklin proposed establishing a circulating subscription library for Philadelphia to members of the Junto.

He described this group in his *Autobiography*:

> *"In the autumn of the preceding year* [1727], *I had form'd most of my ingenious acquaintance into a club of mutual improvement, which we called the Junto; we met on Friday evenings. The rules that I drew up required that every member, in his turn, should produce one or more queries on any point of Morals, Politics, or Natural Philosophy, to be discuss'd by the company; and once in three months produce and read an essay of his own writing, on any subject he pleased. Our debates were to be...conducted in the sincere spirit of inquiry after truth, without fondness for dispute or desire of victory.* [55]

When Franklin proposed to the Junto that they form a subscription library it was an innovation in the American colonies. Colonial America's libraries hitherto were private collections, mostly assembled by and for wealthy men. A circulating subscription library, on other hand, as Franklin envisioned, would be opened to his fellow citizens at large for a fee.

Thus would the quest for knowledge and self-education be served in the larger community, and the establishment of such a library would eventually be understood to foster, nurture and serve democratic ideals.

Franklin's colleagues agreed, and the "Instrument of Association" for the Library Company of Philadelphia was drawn up on July 1, 1731. By November 1731, the Library Company had fifty subscribers, and the first meeting of the library directors was held at Nicholas Scull's Bear Tavern.

Blessed by Franklin's coined motto "To pour forth benefits for the common good is divine," the first—and, until the mid-nineteenth century, the largest—public library in America took root and flourished. Its long and distinguished life included the honor of serving as the Library of Congress when the capital of the young country was located in Philadelphia.

The Library Company flourished and is supported by its shareholders (but open to the public) to this day. It was followed by other membership institutions such as the Boston Athenaeum, which was founded in 1807.

Such associations of friends, neighbors and colleagues formed for purposes of self-improvement, a "spirit of inquiry after truth" and education, like Philadelphia's Junto, were a common feature of eighteenth-century American cities, Salem included. Such associations often took as their mission the improvement of their community's intellectual, moral, social, and educational life.

A Bookish Salem

Salem has been hospitable to books since its earliest days. It has been estimated by one writer that there were approximately a thousand books in Salem as of 1700; the names of bookshops and booksellers abound in early newspapers.

In March 1760, a prominent Salem social club, the Monday Evening Club, met at a popular local tavern and subscribed a fund to establish "a well-chosen library in this Town." And so Salem's Social Library was formed. Shares were available to all who could pay for them, but members were restricted to residence within a circumscribed radius of the city. The Salem Philosophical Library followed in 1781. (These two organizations were the predecessors to the present-day Salem Athenaeum.)[56]

In 1789, John Dabney, a printer and bookseller, and a Salem postmaster began a thirty-year service of providing books that circulated by rental. Rev. William Bentley, who obtained much material from this source, stated that when Dabney opened his first bookstore "anything deserving the name was unknown," but the bookseller "begun as if we were readers of a higher class."

Bentley wrote in 1819 that the "whole town…profitted" from Dabney's bookselling and the circulating library.

Public libraries have existed since classical times; the Great Library of Alexandria, based largely on copies of Aristotle's own collection, is perhaps the most famous library in antiquity.

One consequence of the assassination of Julius Caesar was a delay in building the public library he had planned. Pliny's comment about the library—"He made men's talents a public possession"—was a tribute to both the generosity of the concept and to the services that such a library could provide in a community.

Public–private subscription libraries flourished from the seventeenth to nineteenth century, especially in England and in the United States.

It wasn't until the nineteenth century, however, that the idea of a free and municipally supported library took hold. Founded in 1848, the Boston Public Library holds pride of place as "the first publicly-supported free municipal library in the world."

In Salem, first efforts to establish a free public library met with failure in the early 1870s. However, in 1885, a collection of books was begun with the

The gorgeous springtime face of the Salem Public Library. *Courtesy of author.*

intent of forming such a library. A bequest by the family of sea captain John Bertram, who died on March 22, 1882, provided the collection—and a free, city-supported Salem Public Library—with its permanent home.

The last home the Bertram family inhabited, on Essex Street, is the present-day home to the Salem Public Library, which opened its doors on July 8, 1889. Salem's "Free Public Library" was acknowledged at its founding as providing "incalculable advantages" to the city "and especially to the children and young persons of our community, and to those whose opportunities for education and culture have been limited by the necessities and circumstances of their lives."[57]

Salem's Library Today

Salem's gracefully housed public library is one of the busiest in the North of Boston Library Exchange (NOBLE) system. Like most libraries today, it is home to not only many wonderful books but also to a multimedia center serving the needs of Internet users and movie watchers, researchers of microfilmed documents, and lovers of recorded music.

However, for readers interested in history, it is the Salem Collection and the Salem Room that are most intriguing and useful.

The Salem Collection of books and other materials include concentrations in church history; Salem government; transportation; industry; art, architecture and China trade artifacts; Salem literature and biographies; general Salem histories of various eras; ships and shipmasters; and, of course, the inevitable witchcraft section. There are vertical files, archived newspapers on microfilm, and issues of the Essex Institute Historical Collections to engage the researcher as well.

Most of all, there are the books—ones of great character and personality. It is the charm and the weathered beauty of some of the library's Salem Collection that enchant the most; these travelers from another time call to you as you survey the crowded shelves.

Two devoted reference room librarians at the Salem Public Library, Jane Walsh and Susan Szpak, answered, without hesitation, my interview question, "Why books?"

"Think of the people who handled them," said Szpak. It's that imaginative aspect—the connection to the past, the human connection, which lit up both their faces as they told of the everlasting lure of books. Walsh later added some words that continue to resonate; I'll gift you with them now, in closing.

"I can't imagine a world without books…You can curl up in your favorite spot with a romance and a flashlight in the middle of a thunderstorm. You can surprise a grandchild three thousand miles away with a book he asked Grammie to look for…You can sit in a special collection room of a library and read of daily life in your city or town in the 1850s in a book published by a woman living during that time period. When you hold a book and read, you create a special, private time for yourself."

See you at the library!

"EVERY DOOR IS OPEN TO YOU"—THE ONGOING VOYAGE OF THE PHILLIPS LIBRARY

"Ladies and gentlemen, when our very brief literary and opening exercises are completed, you are not only invited but requested to view the premises completely. Every door is open to you, and members and officials will take pleasure in guiding you." [58]

When General Francis H. Appleton spoke these words to hundreds of members and friends of the Essex Institute on September 9, 1907, he was at once surveying new vistas for the Institute's intellectual, historical and archival work and a new and elegant physical landscape in which to do that work.

The occasion for which Appleton spoke was a grand celebration of the Essex Institute's acquisition of its New Quarters, which was provided by the remodeling and joining of two separate buildings: its previous quarters

An eagle soars above the reading room of the Phillips Library. General Appleton stood on "the bridge" and proclaimed the glories of the new home of the Essex Institute at the 1907 dedication. *Courtesy of author.*

Plummer Hall, circa 1877. *From C.H. Webber and Winfield S. Nevins's* Old Naumkeag: An Historical Sketch of the City of Salem, and the Towns of Marblehead, Peabody, Beverly, Danvers, Wenham, Manchester, Topsfield, and Middleton.

and the adjoining Plummer Hall (where it had, from 1857 to 1905, shared space with the Salem Athenaeum). Plummer Hall, at 134 Essex Street, was originally built with an 1845 bequest to the Athenaeum from Caroline Plummer, given in honor of her brother, Ernestus Augustus.

The site Plummer Hall occupies is also the location of the birthplace of William Hickling Prescott (1796–1859). Prescott's nineteenth-century writings on the conquests of Mexico and Peru are credited with inaugurating serious research in Latin American history in this country. His work, despite current historiographical reassessments, still commands respect today.

The Essex Institute, a privately funded historical society serving Essex County and Salem, traced its roots jointly to 1821, with the birth of the Essex Historical Society, and to 1833, with the formation of the Essex County Natural History Society.

The merging of these two societies in March 1848 resulted in the founding of the Essex Institute, which focused on the collection and preservation of diverse materials for "historical study and teaching in domestic and community life in New England," as an undated Institute brochure describes it.

In particular, the Institute's collections, publications, and activities grew to provide support for those seeking to place the region's history into context both nationally and globally. As it matured, the Institute's collections came to include the James Duncan Phillips Research Library, with 300,000 volumes; thousands of historical manuscripts, photographs, and artistic artifacts; several galleries; and, eventually, historic houses dating from the 1600s to the mid-nineteenth century.

The Institute grew rapidly with predictable results. Periodically, the cry went up for more money and more space.

At the fiftieth anniversary of its founding in March 1898, then President Robert S. Rantoul said, in his commemoration address, that the Institute might have reached a crisis point.

> *Not only valuable books and rare historical papers—the natural accretions of a great library—have been gathered here, but relics and manuscripts and pictures and ancient records—a priceless legacy to the antiquary and the student of local annals, rich material ready to the hand of the historian—have poured in upon us until our receptivity is overtaxed. Buried under the indifference or lost sight of in the greed of the modern Philistine, these relics spared by the tooth of time would have no ministering value to the public; but when rescued...they become...most important parts of a great representative exhibit, picturing as nothing else can do...the actual domestic life of the New England that is gone.*
>
> *The Institute has for twenty-five years, succeeding the Lyceum in the field of oral popular instruction, conducted annual courses of free public lectures... Through its picture and flower and microscope shows, and concerts, and entertainments, it has done its share towards bringing high culture and sound learning and useful knowledge within the reach of everybody.*[59]

But, he went on to say, after more bequests and the ever-increasing scope of its mission, the Institute was pressed against the wall again, literally speaking. "The practical question is this...No room to grow! What will become then of the zeal and enthusiasm of those friends of a lifetime who take a daily pride in our success?"

His *cri de coeur* echoed through the years and, in 1905, the Salem Atheneum sold Plummer Hall to the Essex Institute and built, with the receipts of that sale, its current home at 337 Essex.

At the opening in September 1907 of the conjoined buildings on Essex Street, President Appleton could take much pleasure and pride in the

The Gardner-Pingree House (1805), another Samuel McIntire triumph. Architectural gems such as these gleam everywhere in Salem! *Courtesy of author.*

completely remodeled new home of the Institute as he gave his address from the new balcony that connected the two buildings to the enthusiastic guests below.

He said the Institute must "encourage the opening—broadly—to all uses for which it has been founded...To make known to our citizens that it exists, and, accurately, what it exists for, we ask all who realize that benefits, and helpful pleasure, can come from its patronage, and use...Let it be our pride, and aim...to have the Essex Institute stand a leader in its line of work."[60]

In many areas, the Institute fulfilled his mandate. And in at least a few, it was a pioneer. One of the most intriguing is the installation in 1907 of several unique period rooms.

The concept of a period room in which historical artifacts would be placed in contextually appropriate settings had first begun in European museums; there were several by the end of the nineteenth century. In America, two romanticized exhibits were mounted at the 1876 Philadelphia Centennial: "The Connecticut Cottage" and "Old Log Cabin New England Kitchen," which were furnished with artifacts donated by citizens.

A wonderful place to do research during the few hours it is open; the Phillips Library is both beautiful and inspiring. It's our home away from home in Salem. *Courtesy of author.*

Private collectors also displayed their collections in their homes, sometimes incorporating the woodwork from older buildings into their display areas. In 1904, the Rhode Island School of Design received a gift from Charles L. Pendleton (1849–1904) with the stipulation that his donated collection of decorative arts be housed in a Georgian-style structure, which the school apparently built for the collection. The Metropolitan Museum of Art installed two European period rooms in 1906.

However, the Essex Institute claims pride of place to be the first American museum to utilize period rooms that attempted to portray everyday American life of different eras. This installation was the brainchild of the Institute's secretary, George Francis Dow (1868–1936). The rooms, still open for viewing in the Phillips Library, are set up so it seems as if the occupants had just stepped out from the scene momentarily.

The Essex Institute ceased to exist as a historical society in 1992 when the Peabody Essex Museum in its current incarnation was born. However, the

This is a replica of the original *Salem East Indiaman Friendship*, launched in 1797. It was built and is currently maintained by the National Park Service. A daily delight during walks by the wharf. *Courtesy of author.*

PEM's Phillips Library remains a jewel of unrivaled beauty and unparalleled importance to everyone from ordinary citizens to the scholarly researcher.

Recently retired librarian Britta Karlberg told me in an interview that "Essex County is famous as having the best-documented history in the

United States, and for two hundred years has been collecting documents of everyday life."

Subjects such as sailing vessels, immigrant passenger lists, and photography get much attention from those who utilize the library's holdings. Librarians answer questions online, on the phone, through the mail, and in person during the (painfully restricted) hours the library is open.

Some years ago, I traveled to Cuba on a singing tour. While in Havana, even at its most prestigious library, I was struck and saddened by the dearth of printed materials and other resources evident on every shelf. I remember walking through the stacks, nearly weeping at the deprivation I saw. And, needless to say, what I saw was in sharp contrast to the amazing intellectual riches I have grown up with all my life in the United States. It made me appreciate my access to them all the more.

There is no more precious birthright than free and open access to information.

Deprived of access to libraries such as the Phillips, we are a people without memory. Without the means to understand history, we become prisoners to the moment and incapable of making wise decisions for the future.

Long may our libraries resound to the cry "Every door is open to you!"— and forever may we cherish that right.

Notes

1. PEOPLE

1. List of subscribers who paid for the gateways designed by Samuel McIntire on Salem Common, May 20, 1802, in MSS 0.481, Phillips Library, Peabody Essex Museum, Salem, MA.
2. Fiske Kimball and Essex Institute, *Mr. Samuel McIntire, Carver, the Architect of Salem* (Salem, MA: Essex Institute of Salem, Massachusetts, 1940; repr., Gloucester, MA: Peter Smith, 1966).
3. Dane Morrison and Nancy Lusignan Schultz, eds. *Salem: Place, Myth, and Memory*, UPNE Paperback Edition (Boston: Northeastern University Press, 2005).
4. Arthur W.J.G. Ord-Hume, "Ornamentation in mechanical music," *Early Music* 11, no. 2 (1983).
5. Also note that McIntire's inventory included Handel's *Messiah* in score and a book of *Magdalen Hymns*.
6. Nicholas Temperley, "The Lock Hospital Chapel and Its Music," *Journal of the Royal Musical Association* 118, no. 1 (1993).
7. All Gilmore quotes taken from the massive, entertaining, and utterly amazing P.S. Gilmore, *History of the National Peace Jubilee and Great Musical Festival: Held in the city of Boston, June, 1869, to Commemorate the Restoration of Peace throughout the Land,* (Boston and New York: Lee, Shepard, and Dillingham, 1871).

8. See Chapter CVI: "National Peace Jubilee and Musical Festival, In Boston, In Honor of the Restoration of the Union of the States—1869," in R.M. Devens's *Our first century: Being a popular descriptive portraiture of the one hundred great and memorable events of perpetual interest in the history of our country, political, military, mechanical, social, scientific and commercial: Embracing also delineations of all the great historic characters celebrated in the annals of the republic; men of heroism, statesmanship, genius, oratory, adventure and philanthropy* (Springfield, MA and Easton, PA: C.A. Nichols / J.W. Lyon, 1876), 904–912.

9. Thomas Carroll, "Bands and Band music in Salem," *Essex Institute Historical Collections* 36 (1900).

10. H. Wiley Hitchcock and Kyle Gann, *Music in the United States: A Historical Introduction*, 4th ed. (Alexandria, VA: Prentice Hall, 1999), 133.

11. East Coker Society, "Photos of T.S. Eliot's memorial at St. Michael's Chuch, East Coker," http://www.eastcoker.com/tseliot.html.

12. Information on Elliott's life in Beverly can be found in *Early Records of the town of Beverly* (Beverly, MA: Allen, 1905); "Beverly First Church Records," Essex Historical Collection 35, no. 3 (1899); Essex Institute, *Records of the First Church in Beverly, Mass. 1667–1772*, copied by W.P. Upham (Salem, MA: Essex Institute Historical Collections, 1905).

13. "Native American Deeds," Southern Essex Registry of Deeds, http://www.nativeamericandeeds.com/nativeamericandeedsImage.aspx?q=SalemDeedText3&t=salem.

14. Alfred Poor, "Elliott Genealogy," in Genealogy manuscripts section of the Phillips Library, Salem, MA.

15. Charles Wentworth Upham, *Salem Witchcraft; with an account of Salem Village and a History of Opinions on Witchcraft and Kindred Subjects*, vol. 2, American Classics (New York: F. Ungar,1959), 474–475.

16. Winthrop's writings can be consulted in any number of publications. See the Winthrop Society, "Massachusetts Bay First Settlers—surnames of initial S," in *American History and Genealogy Project* (Auburn, CA: Winthrop Society, 1996–2003); John Winthrop and James Kendall Hosmer, "History of New England," 1630–1649, 2 vols., *Original Narratives of Early American History* (New York: Scribner's, 1908).

17. See entry under "Isaac Stearns," in Henry Bond and Horatio Gates Jones, *Genealogies of the families and descendants of the early settlers of Watertown, Massachusetts, including Waltham and Weston; to which is appended the early history of the town. With illustrations, maps, and notes. With a memoir of the author by Horatio Gates Jones A.M.*, 2nd ed., vol. 2. (Boston: N.E. Historic-Genealogical Society, 1860).

18. Ibid.

19. Nan Webber, "Literary Gloucester: T.S. Eliot in Gloucester," Valentine Design and Parlez-Moi Press, http://www.valentine-design.com/Literary/eliot.htm.

20. Donald Hall, "The Art of Poetry No. 1: T.S. Eliot," *Paris Review* (1959).

21. John J. Soldo, "The American Foreground of T.S. Eliot," *New England Quarterly* 45, no. 3 (1972).

22. "Gentlemen and Seamen," originally published in the *Harvard Advocate* 87, no. 115 (May 1909); see Donald Hall, *The Harvard Advocate Anthology*, Essay Index Reprint Series (Freeport, NY: Books for Libraries Press, 1970).

23. The Londoner's Diary, "T.S Eliot widow loses grip on private papers," *The Evening Standard*, August 15, 1993, page 4.

24. Nicholas E. Tawa, *Arthur Foote: A Musician in the Frame of Time and Place*, Composers of North America Series (Lanham, MD: Scarecrow Press, 1997).

25. See entries for dates mentioned, and supplemental notes by daughter Mary Wilder (Foote) Tileston, in Mary Wilder Tileston et al., *Caleb and Mary Wilder Foote* (Boston and New York: Houghton Mifflin, 1918).

26. Arthur Foote, Moses Smith, and Frederick Jacobi, *Arthur Foote, 1853–1937. An Autobiography* (Norwood, MA: Plimpton, 1946).

27. Arthur Foote, "A Bostonian Remembers," *Musical Quarterly* 23, no. 1 (1937).

28. Tawa, *Arthur Foote*, 362–363

29. James R. Mellow, *Nathaniel Hawthorne in His Times*, Johns Hopkins Paperback Edition (Baltimore, MD: Johns Hopkins University Press, 1998), 293, 325.

30. "The Hawthornes in Lenox. Told in letters by Sophia Hawthorne, (Herman Melville, and Others.) edited by Rose Hawthorne Lathrop," *Century* (1895).

31. Elizabeth Donnan and Carnegie Institution of Washington, *Documents Illustrative of the History of the Slave Trade to America*, 4 vols., Carnegie Institution of Washington. (Washington, DC: Carnegie Institution of Washington, 1930), v3, 3.

32. Joel Lang, "Chapter One: The Plantation Next Door; How Salem Slaves, Wethersfield Onions and West Indies Sugar Made Connecticut Rich," *Hartford Courant*, http://courant.com/news/specials/hcplantation.artsep29,0,6363125.story.

33. Nathaniel Hawthorne, "Browne's Folly," *The Dolliver Romance, and Other Pieces*. (Boston and New York: Houghton, 1904).

34. "Family connections to the Royall House," Royall House Association, http://www.royallhouse.org/geneology.php.

35. Timothy Fitch and Peter Gwinn, "*The Medford Slave Trade Letters 1759–1765*," Medford Historical Society, http://medfordhistorical.org/slavetradeletters.php.
36. Elizabeth Donnan, "The New England Slave Trade After the Revolution," *New England Quarterly* 3, no. 2 (1930).
37. Robert E. Desrochers Jr., "Slave-for-sale Advertisements and Slavery in Massachusetts, 1704–1781," *William and Mary Quarterly* 59, no. 3 (2002).
38. Joseph Barlow Felt, *Annals of Salem*, 2nd ed., 2 vols. (Salem and Boston: W&SB Ives / James Munroe, 1849), 416; 247.
39. Calvin Lane, "The African Squadron: The U.S. Navy and the Slave Trade," Mystic Seaport, Mystic, CT, http://amistad.mysticseaport.org.
40. Margaret H. Bacon, *The Quiet Rebels; the Story of the Quakers in America*, Culture & Discovery Books (New York: Basic Books, 1969), 30–31.
41. Marcus Rediker, "Slavery: A shark's perspective; a strange text sheds new light on the true roots of abolition," *Boston Globe*, September 23, 2007, http://www.boston.com/news/globe/ideas/articles/2007/09/23/slavery_a_sharks_perspective/.
42. Jonathan Saunders, "Notes on town meeting: Resolved, that in the opinion of this meeting...By all practical means to prevent the extension of so great a political and moral evil as slavery," 1819, in handwritten manuscript, notes of town meeting; Collection of Robert Booth, 3 pages, Phillips Library, Salem, MA. Also see "Town meeting (on extension of slavery); old opinions on slavery," *Salem Gazette*, Friday morning, December 10, 1819.
43. Beth A. Salerno, *Sister Societies: Women's Antislavery Organizations in Antebellum America* (DeKalb: Northern Illinois University Press, 2005).

2. CULTURE THEN AND NOW

44. Broadside in the ephemera collections, Phillips Library, Salem, MA.
45. Sydney E. Ahlstrom, *A Religious History of the American People* (New Haven, CT: Yale University Press, 1972).
46. See chapter 2, "Great Mediums from 1870 to 1900: Charles H. Foster-Madame d'Esperance-Eglinton-Stainton Moses," in Arthur Conan Doyle, *The History of Spiritualism*, vol. 2 (London and New York: Cassel, 1926).
47. Robert C. Fuller, *Mesmerism and the American Cure of Souls* (Philadelphia: University of Pennsylvania Press, 1982), 44, 46.

48. Francis Higginson et al., *New-englands plantation: With the Sea Journal and Other Writings*, Publications of the Essex Book and Print Club No. 1 (Salem, MA: Essex Book and Print Club, 1908), 107.
49. Richard D. Brown and Jack Tager, *Massachusetts: A Concise History*, Revised and Expanded Edition (Amherst: University of Massachusetts Press, 2000), 173.
50. John Frayler, "Ethnic backgrounds and occupational trends among immigrants to Salem, MA. Originally researched for a discussion presentation by John Frayler, May 5, 1988," typescript, Salem Public Library, Salem, MA.
51. Roy Flukinger and Barbara Brown, "Joseph Nicéphore Niépce and the First Photograph," Harry Ransom Center at the University of Texas at Austin, http://www.hrc.utexas.edu/exhibitions/permanent/wfp/.
52. James M. Lindgren, "'That every mariner may possess the history of the world': A Cabinet for the East India Marine Society of Salem," *New England Quarterly* 68, no. 2 (1995).
53. Amy Ione, "Review: Time stands still: Muybridge and the instantaneous photography movement by Phillip Prodger," *Leonardo* 36, no. 5 (2003).
54. T. Frederick Hardwich, *A Manual of Photographic Chemistry: Including the Practice of the Collodion Process*, 4th. ed. (London: J. Churchill, 1857), 288.

3. LEGACY LOCATIONS

55. Benjamin Franklin and H. Hastings Weld, *Benjamin Franklin: His Autobiography; with a narrative of his public life and services* (New York: J.C. Derby, 1855), 103. See also the Library Company's website at http://www.librarycompany.org/.
56. Harriet Silvester Tapley and Essex Institute, *Salem Imprints, 1768–1825: A History of the First fifty Years of Printing in Salem, Massachusetts with some account of the bookshops, booksellers, bookbinders and the private libraries* (Salem, MA: Essex Institute, 1927).
57. Aida Butler, "The Historical Evolution of libraries in Salem, Massachusetts 1760–1970," typescript, Salem Public Library, Salem, MA.
58. *Salem Evening News*, "New Quarters of Institute Seen—New Building Made of Old Institute Building and Plummer Hall seen by Members and Friends Last Night; Gen. Francis Appleton spoke; Several hundred present," September 10, 1907 (See also related story, September 7, 1907, with illustration of Hall).

NOTES TO PAGES 117–118

59. "The First Half Century of the Essex Institute," *Bulletin of the Essex Institute* 30 (Salem, MA: Essex Institute, 1898), 6–7.

60. *Salem Evening News*, "New Quarters of Institute Seen—New Building Made of Old Institute Building and Plummer Hall seen by Members and Friends Last Night; Gen. Francis Appleton spoke; Several hundred present," September 10, 1907.

Selected Bibliography

The full bibliography for this book (drawn from researching the *Gazette*'s Naumkeag Notations columns) runs to nearly four hundred entries (with nearly as many footnotes). Due to publishing space constraints, I couldn't include them all and still have room for the Stories and Shadows.

So, I decided to give you a selected bibliography, largely for sources not named in the endnotes or text itself. If, however, you'd like the full list of sources I consulted for these chapters, please write to me! You can find me at http://singingstring.org or at the Institute's website at http://imhct.org.

Chapter 1: People

"Distinguished for Genius" Musical Mr. McIntire

Downs, Joseph. "Derby and McIntire." *The Metropolitan Museum of Art Bulletin* 6, no. 2 (1947): 73-80.

"The Foundling Hospital and Its Music." *The Musical Times and Singing Class Circular* 43, no. 711 (1902): 304-311.

"George Washington's Mount Vernon Estate and Gardens: History of Mount Vernon." Mount Vernon Ladies Association. http://www.mountvernon.org/learn/explore_mv/index.cfm/ss/27/.

Lahikainen, Dean T. and Peabody Essex Museum. *Samuel McIntire: Carving an American Style*. Distributed by University Press of New England, 2007.

Lloyd, Sarah. "Pleasing Spectacles and Elegant Dinners: Conviviality, Benevolence, and Charity Anniversaries in Eighteenth-Century London." *Journal of British Studies* 41: 23–57.

———. "'Pleasure's Golden Bait': Prostitution, Poverty and the Magdalen Hospital in Eighteenth-Century London." *History Workshop Journal*, no. 41 (1996): 50-70.

McCutchan, Robert G. "American Church Music Composers of the Early Nineteenth Century." *Church History* 2, no. 3 (1933): 139–151.

Musical Times and Singing Class Circular 8, no. 182. "The Foundling Hospital" (1858): 220.

Nash, Stanley. "Prostitution and Charity: The Magdalen Hospital, a Case Study." *Journal of Social History* 17, no. 4 (1984): 617–628.

Salem Gazette. "For Sale, Sundry Articles Belonging to the Estate of Samuel Mcintire, Deceased." Tuesday, April 30, 1811.

Simon, McVeigh. "Music and Lock Hospital in the 18th Century." *Musical Times* 129, no. 1743 (1988): 235–240.

Temperley, Nicholas. "The Lock Hospital Chapel and Its Music." *Journal of the Royal Musical Association* 118, no. 1 (1993): 44–72.

Patrick Gilmore: Romancing the Angel

"The Boston Peace Jubilee." *Harper's Weekly*, Saturday, June 19, 1869.

"The Boston Peace Musical Festival." *Musical Times and Singing Class Circular* 14, no. 318 (1869): 172–173.

Cipolla, Frank J. "Patrick S. Gilmore: The Boston Years." *American Music* 6, no. 3 (1988): 281–292.

Dalton, James B. *Gilmore's Road to Salem: The Fiddle Tune, The Irish Bandmaster, and the Winter Island Muster*. Salem, MA: Institute for Music, History and Cultural Traditions, Inc., as part of the American History and Music Project, May 23, 2010. Multimedia (illustrated lecture–performance).

Damon, Frank C. Clippings used in 1930s *Salem News* Series on Patrick S. Gilmore. Also contains undated ephemera, photos. Phillips Library, Salem, MA.

Gilmore, Stephen. "Patrick Sarsfield Gilmore: America's Prototypical Impresario." *Journal of Band Research* (Fall 1998) 34: 69–100.

Jarman, Rufus. "Big Boom in Boston." October 1969. American Heritage, http://www.americanheritage.com/articles/magazine/ah/1969/6/1969_6_46.shtml (accessed 2007).

Newsom, Jon. "The American Brass Band Movement: A Historical Overview." Library of Congress, Music Division, Washington, D.C. http://memory.loc.gov/ammem/cwmhtml/cwmhome.html (accessed April 14, 2007).

Patrick Gilmore Collection. Performing Arts Library, University of Maryland, Clarice Smith Performing Arts Center, College Park, Maryland. http://hdl.handle.net/1903.1/1214 (accessed 2007).

"At the Source of the Longest River"—T.S. Eliot's Salem Roots

Carlson, C.C., and North Shore Community College. "Eastern Point (Gloucester Harbor) Location, History, and Legends." Poetry of Places in Essex County, http://myweb.northshore.edu/users/ccarlsen/poetry/gloucester/easternpointhistory.htm (accessed February 18, 2008).

Donoghue, Denis "T.S. Eliot and the Poem Itself." *The Partisan Review*, June 5, 2000.

Eliot, Thomas Stearns. "The Sacred Wood; Essays on Poetry and Criticism" July 1996 by Bartleby.com, http://www.bartleby.com/200/sw4.html (accessed February 2, 2008).

———. "The Waste Land." February 1998 by Bartleby.com, http://www.bartleby.com/201/1.html (accessed February 18, 2008).

Eliot, T.S. *Four Quartets*. The Centenary ed. San Diego, CA: Harcourt, Brace, Jovanovich, 1988.

———. *Selected Poems*, New York: Harcourt, Brace, Jovanovich, 1964.

Eliot, T.S., and Frank Kermode. *Selected Prose of T.S. Eliot*. New York: Harcourt, Brace, Jovanovich / Farrar, Straus, and Giroux, 1975.

Ellis, P.G. "The Development of T.S. Eliot's Historical Sense." *Review of English Studies* 23, no. 91 (1972): 291–301.

A Guide to Stearns Family Papers, 1714–1920. Special Collections, Virginia Polytechnic Institute and State University, Blacksburg, VA. http://ead.lib.virginia.edu/vivaead/published/vt/viblbv00149.document (Accessed February 10, 2008).

"The Influence of Landscape Upon the Poet. (Speech made by T.S. Eliot) (Includes related article on psychological history)(American Academic Culture in Transformation: Fifty Years, Four Disciplines)(Transcript)." *Daedalus* 126, no. 1 (1997): 353–5.

"John Winthrop: 'A Modell of Christian Charity' (1630)." ABC-CLIO. http://www.americanhistory.abc-clio.com.(accessed March 1, 2008)

"The Last Puritan." *Time* (1941). Reprinted on http://www.time.com/time/printout/0,8816,795201,00.html (accessed February 4, 2008).

"Reflections: Mr. Eliot." *Time* (March 6, 1950). Reprinted on http://www.time.com/time/magazine/article0,9171,858646,00.html (accessed February 4, 2008).

Stone, Edwin M. *History of Beverly, Civil and Ecclesiastical, From Its Settlement in 1630 to 1842*. Boston: James Munroe, 1843. Reprint, 1975.

A Life Lived in Harmony: Composer Arthur Foote

Hubbard, William Lines, George W. Andrews, Edward Dickinson, Arthur William Foote, Janet M. Green, Josephine Thrall, and Emil Liebling. *American History and Encyclopedia of Music*. 12 vols. Toledo, New York: I. Squire, 1908.

Knight, Ellen E. *Charles Martin Loeffler: A Life Apart in American Music*, Music in American Life. Urbana: University of Illinois Press, 1992.

Lane, Edith. "Arthur Foote: Massachusetts' Own Musician." Manuscripts. Phillips Library, Salem, MA.

Mason, Redfern. "The Passing of Arthur Foote." *Boston Evening Transcript*, April 17, 1937, page 6.

"Mrs. Mary F. Foote." *Salem Gazette*, December 29, 1857.

Smith-Dalton, Margaret R. *History, Harmony, and Headlines: The Footes of Salem, Music, and The Salem Gazette*. June 2, 2010. Institute for Music, History, and Cultural Traditions, Inc. as part of the American History and Music Project. Multimedia (illustrated lecture–performance).

Tawa, Nicholas E. *Arthur Foote: A Musician in the Frame of Time and Place*. Composers of North America series. Lanham, MD: Scarecrow Press, 1997.

———. *From Psalm to Symphony: a History of Music in New England*. Boston: Northeastern University Press, 2001.

Summer Storms, Story Novelists: Hawthorne and Melville

Atlantic Monthly: A Magazine of Literature, Science, Art, and Politics 93 (1903 and 1904).

Clark, C.E. Frazer Jr. "Origins of the American Renaissance: A Front-Page Story." *Studies in the American Renaissance* (1977): 155–164.

Hawthorne, Julian. *Nathaniel Hawthorne and His Wife: A Biography*. vol. 2. Boston and New York: Houghton, Mifflin / Riverside Press, Cambridge, 1891.

———. *Hawthorne and His Circle*. New York and London: Harper & Brothers, 1903.

Hawthorne, Julian and Edith Garrigues Hawthorne. *The Memoirs of Julian Hawthorne*. New York: Macmillan, 1938.

"The Hawthornes in Lenox. Told in Letters by Sophia Hawthorne, (Herman Melville, and others.) Edited by Rose Hawthorne Lathrop." *Century* (1895), 86–98.

Hoeltje, Hubert H. "The Writing of the Scarlet Letter." *New England Quarterly* 27, no. 3 (1954): 326–346.

Lathrop, Rose Hawthorne. *Memories of Hawthorne*. Boston and New York: Houghton Mifflin / Riverside Press, 1897.

Leverenz, David. *Manhood and the American Renaissance*. Ithaca, NY: Cornell University Press, 1989.

Minnigerode, Meade and Herman Melville. *Some Personal Letters of Herman Melville and a Bibliography*. New York: E.B. Hackett / Brick Row Book Shop, 1922.

"Nathaniel Hawthorne." March 1, 2008. ABC-CLIO. http://www.americanhistory.abc-clio.com.

Phillips, John A. "Melville meets Hawthorne." December 1975. American Heritage http://www.americanheritage.com/articles/magazine/ah/1975/1/1975_1_16.shtml.

Rose Hawthorne Lathrop Papers. Finding aid. The Dominican Sisters of Hawthorne. http://www.hawthorne-dominicans.org/archvs.htm.

Whitney, Terri, and Sandra Carriker. "Hawthorne in Salem (N.E.H. Project: Hawthorne in the Museum and in the Classroom)." North Shore Community College, Danvers, MA; Peabody Essex Museum, House of the Seven Gables Historic Site and Salem Maritime National Historic Site, Salem, MA. http://www.hawthorneinsalem.org/page/10002/ (accessed May 30, 2010).

Salem Navigates the Tides of Reform: Abolition and Slavery

"Anti-slavery Operations of the US Navy: Images from Publications in the Navy Department Library." Department of the Navy. http://www.history.navy.mil/library/special/slavetrade.htm.

Bennett, Norman R. Jr. and George E. Brooks. *New England Merchants in Africa: A History Through Documents, 1802-1865*, African Research Studies, no. 7. Brookline, MA: Boston University Press, 1965.

Blanck, Emily. "Seventeen Eighty-Three: The Turning Point in the Law of Slavery and Freedom in Massachusetts." *New England Quarterly* 75, no. 1 (2002): 24–51.

Brown, William W. *The Anti-Slavery Harp: A Collection of Songs for Anti-Slavery Meetings.* Boston: Bela Marsh, 1849.

"By Authority of Congress: The Public Statutes at Large of the United States of America from the Organization of the Government in 1789 to March 3, 1845. Arranged in Chronological Order. With References to the Matter of Each Act and to the Subsequent Acts on the Same Subject, and Copious Notes of the Decisions of the Courts of the United States," in *Exploring Amistad at Mystic Seaport: 1807 U.S. Law on Slave Trade* by Richard Peters, esq. http://amistad.mysticseaport.org/library/govt.papers/legis/1807.act.barss (accessed May 27, 2008).

Caswell, Michelle. "Caswell: Why Visit the Royall House, Slave Quarters?" *Medford Transcript*, April 8, 2008.

Collison, Gary L. "Alexander Burton and Salem's "Fugitive Slave Riot" of 1851." *Essex Institute Historical Collections* 128, no. 1 (1992): 17–26.

"Constitution of the Salem Female Anti-Slavery Society." Box 1. Anti-Slavery Society of Salem and Vicinity Records, 1834–1840; 1886. Phillips Library, Salem, MA.

De Fontaine, F.G. *History of American abolitionism; its four great epochs, embracing narratives of the ordinance of 1787, compromise of 1820, annexation of Texas, Mexican war, Wilmot proviso, negro insurrections, abolition riots, slave rescues, compromise of 1850, Kansas bill of 1854, John Brown insurrection, 1859, valuable statistics, &c., &c., &c., together with a history of the southern confederacy.* New York: D. Appleton, 1861.

Eltis, David. "The Nineteenth-Century Transatlantic Slave Trade: An Annual Time Series of Imports into the Americas Broken down by Region." *Hispanic American Historical Review* 67, no. 1 (1987): 109–138.

Fickes, Michael L. ""They Could Not Endure That Yoke': The Captivity of Pequot Women and Children after the War of 1637." *New England Quarterly* 73, no. 1 (2000): 58–81.

Goodell, William. *Slavery and Anti-Slavery; a History of the Great Struggle in Both Hemispheres; with a View of the Slavery Question in the United States.* New York: W. Harned, 1852.

Greene, Lorenzo Johnston. *The Negro in Colonial New England.* Studies in American Negro Life. New York: Atheneum, 1968.

Heuman, Gad J. and James Walvin. *The Slavery Reader.* London and New York: Routledge, 2003.

Jeffrey, Julie Roy. "Permeable Boundaries: Abolitionist Women and Separate Spheres." *Journal of the Early Republic* 21, no. 1 (2001): 79–93.

Lane, Calvin. "Joseph Story." Mystic Seaport, Mystic, CT. http://amistad. mysticseaport.org (accessed April 14, 2008).

Leon, F. Litwack. "The Abolitionist Dilemma: The Antislavery Movement and the Northern Negro." *New England Quarterly* 34, no. 1 (1961): 50–73.

Linebaugh, Peter and Marcus Buford Rediker. *The Many-Headed Hydra: Sailors, Slaves, Commoners, and the Hidden History of the Revolutionary Atlantic.* Boston: Beacon Press, 2000.

Lydia Maria Francis Child Papers, 1835–1894. William L. Clements Library, University of Michigan. http://quod.lib.umich.edu/cgi/f/findaid/findaid-idx?c=clementsmss;cc=clementsmss;q1=Child%2C%20Lydia%20Maria;rgn=Entire%20Finding%20Aid;view=text;didno=umich-wcl-M-1497chi (accessed April 7, 2008).

MacQuarrie, Brian. "A Clash Over Marking Winthrop's Slave Past." *Boston Globe*, April 10, 2000, third edition.

———. "Out of the Past in Winthrop, Residents Clash Over Marking Slavery History." *Boston Globe*, April 17, 2000, third edition.

Mason, Matthew E. "Slavery Overshadowed: Congress Debates Prohibiting the Atlantic Slave Trade to the United States, 1806-1807." *Journal of the Early Republic* 20, no. 1 (2000): 59–81.

McKivigan, John R. and Mary O'Brien Gibson. "A Brief History of the American Abolitionist Movement." Indiana University–Purdue University and the trustees of Indiana University. Indianapolis, IN. American Abolitionism. http://americanabolitionist.liberalarts.iupui.edu/brief.htm (accessed May 20, 2008).

McManus, Edgar J. *Black Bondage in the North.* 1st ed. Syracuse, NY: Syracuse University Press, 1973.

Newmyer, R. Kent. *Supreme Court Justice Joseph Story: Statesman of the Old Republic.* Studies in Legal History. Chapel Hill: University of North Carolina Press, 1985.

Ostrander, Gilman M. "The Making of the Triangular Trade Myth." *William and Mary Quarterly* 30, no. 4 (1973): 635-644.

Perley, Sidney. "Chapter II: The Game Preserve." 2002. The History of Salem, Massachusetts. http://etext.virginia.edu/salem/witchcraft/Perley (accessed April 20, 2008).

Price, David A. "Remembering the Jamestown Colony After 400 Years: Year In Review 2007." Encyclopaedia Britannica Online. http://www.britannica.com/EBchecked/topic/1384525/Remembering-the-Jamestown-Colony-After-400-Years (accessed April 17, 2008).

Rediker, Marcus. "Slavery: A Shark's Perspective; A Strange Text Sheds New Light on the True Roots of Abolition." *Boston Globe*, September 23, 2007.
————. *The Slave Ship: A Human History*. New York: Viking, 2007.
Roediger, David R. and Martin Henry Blatt. *The Meaning of Slavery in the North*. Garland Reference Library of Social Science. New York: Garland, 1998.
"Slavery in Massachusetts; Extent and Importance of the Colonial Slave Trade." *Boston Globe*, July 29, 1883.
"Slavery [Report on Town Meeting of Previous Day]." *Essex Register*, Wednesday, December 8, 1819, page 3.
Sokolow, Michael. "'New Guinea at One End, and a View of the Alms-House at the Other': The Decline of Black Salem, 1850-1920." *New England Quarterly* 71, no. 2 (1998): 204–228.
Story, Joseph and William Wetmore Story. *The Miscellaneous Writings of Joseph Story*. Boston: C.C. Little and J. Brown, 1852.
Story, William Wetmore. *Life and Letters of Joseph Story, Associate Justice of the Supreme Court of the United States, and Dane Professor of Law at Harvard University*. Boston: C.C. Little and J. Brown, 1851.
"A Timeline of Events and References Leading Up To and Through the Founding of Jamestown." Preservation Virginia and Historic Jamestowne, Jamestown, VA. http://www.preservationvirginia.org/rediscovery/page.php?page_id=29 (accessed April 21, 2008).
Tytler, J. *The rising of the sun in the west: or The origin and progress of liberty / By J. Tytler—one of the compilers of the Encyclopoedia Britannica in Scotland.—Exiled from that country, on account of his writings in the cause of liberty, Jan. 7th 1793, and lately arrived in America from Belfast in Ireland.; Composed during the voyage*. Salem, MA: William Carlton, 1795.
"The United States Navy and the Slave Trade." Mel Fisher Maritime Museum, Key West, FL. http://www.melfisher.org/exhibitions/lastslaveships/ (accessed April 14, 2008).

CHAPTER 2: CULTURE THEN AND NOW

Salem's Psychic Past Lives

"Are the Phenomena of Spiritualism Supernatural?" *New Englander and Yale Review* (May 1860), 381–412.
American Spiritual Magazine. Vol. 3. Edited by S. Watson. Memphis, TN: Southern Baptist Publication Society, 1877.

Brink, Carol Ryrie. *Harps in the Wind: The Story of the Singing Hutchinsons*. Da Capo Press Music Reprint Series. New York: Da Capo Press, 1980.

Britten, Emma Hardinge. *Modern American Spiritualism: Twenty Years' Record of the Communion between Earth and the World of Spirits*. 4th ed. New York: Emma Hardinge Britten, 1870.

Davies, Owen. "Charmers and charming in England and Wales from the Eighteenth to the Twentieth century." *Folklore* 109 (1998): 41.

DeSalvo, John. "Andrew Jackson Davis; the First American Prophet and Clairvoyant." http://www.andrewjacksondavis.com/ (accessed 2007).

Doyle, Arthur Conan. *The Vital Message*. New York: George H. Doran, 1919.

Drabelle, Dennis. "Feet and Faith." *Pennsylvania Gazette*, March–April 2006, http://www.upenn.edu/gazette/0306/feature2.html.

Fuller, Robert C. *Mesmerism and the American Cure of Souls*. Philadelphia: University of Pennsylvania Press, 1982.

Home, D.D. *Lights and Shadows of Spiritualism*. 2nd ed. London: Virtue, 1878.

James, Henry. "Spiritualism New and Old." *Atlantic* (March 1872), 358–362.

Kerr, Howard and Charles L. Crow. *The Occult in America: New Historical Perspectives*. Urbana: University of Illinois Press, 1983.

"Modern Spiritualism." *Putnam's Monthly Magazine of American Literature, Science and Art* (January 1, 1853), 59–64.

Packard, J.B. and J.S. Loveland. *The Spirit Minstrel; a Collection of Hymns and Music, for the Use of Spiritualists, in Their Circles and Public Meetings*. 2nd ed. Boston: Bela Marsh, 1856.

Polidoro, M. "Anna Eva Fay: The Mentalist Who Baffled Sir William Crookes." *Skeptical Inquirer* (2000).

"Preliminary Report of the Commission Appointed by The University of Pennsylvania to Investigate Modern Spiritualism in Accordance with the Bequest of the Late Henry Seybert." Philadelphia: J.B. Lippincott, 1887.

Roach, Paul. "Wandering Between Two Worlds: Victorian England's Search for Meaning." September 28,1999. http://webcache.googleusercontent.com/search?q=cache:v24Nhe0uXBoJ:www.aiprinc.org/para-c01_Roach_1999.doc+Wandering+Between+Two+Worlds:+Victorian+England%27s+Search+for+Meaning&cd=1&hl=en&ct=clnk&gl=us&client=firefox-a. (accessed 2006).

Simanek, Donald E. "Arthur Conan Doyle, Spiritualism, and Fairies." Lock Haven University. http://www.lhup.edu/~dsimanek/doyle.htm (accessed 2006).

If Music Be The Food Of Love: Historic Foodways of Salem

Beecher, Catharine Esther and Harriet Beecher Stowe. *The American woman's home; or, Principles of domestic science; being a guide to the formation and maintenance of economical, healthful, beautiful, and Christian homes.* Edited by and with a new introduction by Joseph Van Why. 3rd ed. Hartford, CT: Stowe-Day Foundation, 1985. Reprint, 1975.

"Dyspepsia, or....Indigestion." *Salem Gazette*, October 21, 1828, page 4.

Elvey, George J. "Thanksgiving Day." The *Hymnal of the Protestant Episcopal Church in the United States of America, 1940.* Vol. 2. New York: Church Pension Fund, 1943.

Gardapee, Pamela "How to Make Dyspepsia Bread." eHow.com, http://www.ehow.com/PrintArticle.html?id=2303531

Hale, Sarah Josepha Buell. *The way to live well and to be well while we live; containing directions for choosing and preparing food, in regard to health, economy and taste.* Boston: H. Wentworth, 1851.

Mann, Mary Tyler Peabody. *Christianity in the Kitchen: A Physiological Cook Book*, by Mrs. Horace Mann. Boston: Ticknor and Fields, 1857.

McWilliams, James E. *A Revolution in Eating: How the Quest for Food Shaped America.* Arts and Traditions of the Table. New York: Columbia University Press, 2005.

Smith-Dalton, Margaret R. "A Nibble or Two on Early Foodways in New England and Salem." November 11, 2008. Multimedia (illustrated lecture).

Stavely, Keith W.F. and Kathleen Fitzgerald. *America's Founding Food: the Story of New England Cooking.* Chapel Hill: University of North Carolina Press, 2004.

What Salem Dames Cooked; Being a Choice Collection of Recipes where is shewn how The Delectable Practice of the Salem Dames from the year 1683, to 1730, until 1800 and 1900, may be restored with pleasure to those desirous of experiencing The Delights of their Cookery, together with A Few Housekeeping Hints and Numerous Appropriate Quotations. Boston: Station Press, 1911.

"Céad Mile Failte": The Green Fields of America (Irish in Salem)

Appel, John J. "The New England Origins of the American Irish Historical Society." *New England Quarterly* 33, no. 4 (1960): 462–475.

Beirne, Hilary. "The History of New York City St. Patrick's Day Parade." St Patrick's Day Parade & Celebration Committee, Bronx, NY. http://nyc-st-patrick-day-parade.org/paradehistory.aspx (accessed 2007).

"Celebrating Irish-American Heritage Month." American Foundation for Irish Heritage, Washington, D.C. http://www.irishamericanheritage.com/webpageirish1.htm (accessed March 19, 2007).

Dunne, W.M.P. "An Irish Immigrant Success Story." *New England Quarterly* 65, no. 2 (1992): 284–290.

Flagg, Charles Allcott. *A guide to Massachusetts local history : being a bibliographic index to the literature of the towns, cities and counties of the state, including books, pamphlets, articles in periodicals and collected works, books in preparation, historical manuscripts, newspaper clippings, etc.* Salem, MA: Salem Press, 1907.

Joyce, P.W. "A Concise History of Ireland, Part V; The Period of the Penal Laws 1695-1829." Library Ireland. http://www.libraryireland.com/JoyceHistory/PartV.php (accessed 2007).

McGee, Thomas D'Arcy. *A history of the Irish settlers in North America from the earliest period to the census of 1850.* 2nd ed. Boston: Patrick Donahoe, 1852.

———. "The Irish in Massachusetts." In *A History of the Irish Settlers in North America*: Library Ireland. http://www.libraryireland.com/IrishSettlers/Massachusetts.php (accessed 2007).

Morris, Richard J. "Urban Population in Revolutionary America: The Case of Salem, Massachusetts 1759-1799." *Journal of Urban History* 9, no. 1: 3–30.

O'Brien, Michael Joseph. "The Pioneer Irish of Essex County." *American Irish Historical Journal* 26 (1927).

"Profile of General Demographic Characteristics: 2000." U.S. Census Bureau.

Quinn, John F. "Father Mathew's Disciples: American Catholic Support for Temperance, 1840–1920." *Church History* 65, no. 4 (1996): 624–640.

Ring, Michael J. "Evaluating Evacuation Day: St. Patrick's Day Might Be a Celebration of Immigration." *Tech* (MIT). http://tech.mit.edu/V118/N14/ring.14c.html.

"Salem City, Massachusetts QuickLinks." U.S. Census Bureau. http://quickfacts.census.gov/qfd/states/25/2559105.html.

Schaffer, Patricia. "Laws in Ireland for the suppression of Popery commonly known as the Penal Laws." University of Minnesota Law School, Minneapolis, MN. http://library.law.umn.edu/irishlaw/intro.html.

Singer, David. "Hawthorne and the 'Wild Irish': A Note." *New England Quarterly* 42, no. 3 (1969): 425–432.

Walsh, Louis Sebastian. *Origin of the Catholic Church in Salem, and its growth in St. Mary's parish and the parish of the Immaculate Conception.* Boston: Cashman, Keating, 1890.

Substance and Shadow: Photography at the PEM

"Analyzing the World's First Photograph: Precious Image Studied at Getty Institute in Los Angeles." *Weekend All Things Considered, National Public Radio.* April 7, 2002. http://www.npr.org/programs/watc/features/2002/mar/photograph/

Flukinger, Roy and Barbara Brown. "Joseph Nicéphore Niépce and the First Photograph." Harry Ransom Center at the University of Texas at Austin, Austin, TX. http://www.hrc.utexas.edu/exhibitions/permanent/wfp/ (accessed 2009).

Nickel, Douglas R. "History of Photography: The State of Research." *Art Bulletin* 83, no. 3 (2001): 548–558.

Painter, Nell Irvin. *Sojourner Truth: A Life, A Symbol.* New York: W.W. Norton, 1997.

Ribemont, F., Patrick Daum, Phillip Prodger, St. Louis Art Museum, and Musée des beaux-arts de Rennes. *Impressionist Camera: Pictorial Photography in Europe, 1888-1918.* Illustrated ed. Ann Arbor: University of Michigan, 2006; Digitized Dec 17, 2007.

"Timeline of the Daguerreian Era." Library of Congress, Washington, D.C. http://memory.loc.gov/ammem/daghtml/dagtime.html (accessed 2009).

Trachtenberg, Alan. *Reading American Photographs: Images as History, Mathew Brady to Walker Evans.* 1st ed. New York: Hill and Wang, 1989.

CHAPTER 3: LEGACY LOCATIONS

"Incalculable Advantages"—Salem's Public Library

"Boston Public Library: A Brief History and Description." Boston Public Library, Boston, MA. http://bpl.org/general/history.htm (accessed 2007).

Butler, Aida. "The Historical Evolution of Libraries in Salem, Massachusetts 1760-1970." Article. Salem Public Library, Salem, MA.

Franklin, Benjamin, and H. Hastings Weld. *Benjamin Franklin: His Autobiography; with a narrative of his public life and services.* New York: J.C. Derby, 1855.

Little, Selina F. "Salem Public Library; History of the Building." Salem Public Library, Salem, MA. http://www.noblenet.org/salem/library/history.html (accessed May 2007).

Parton, James. *Life and times of Benjamin Franklin.* 2 vols. New York and Boston: Mason Brothers / Mason & Hamlin, 1864.

Shera, Jesse Hauk. *Foundations of the Public Library; the Origins of the Public Library Movement in New England, 1629-1855.* Hamden, CT: Shoe String Press, 1965.

Walsh, Jane. Brief letters to the author. April 23-24, 2007.

"Every Door Is Open to You":
The Ongoing Voyage of the Phillips Library

Corning, Howard. "The Essex Institute of Salem." *Bulletin of the Business Historical Society* 7, no. 5 (1933): 1–5.

Dalton, Tom. "PEM hires director for Phillips Library." *Salem News*, February 13, 2007.

James Duncan Phillips Library. Peabody Essex Museum, Salem, MA. http://www.pem.org/library

Pilgrim, Dianne H. "Inherited from the Past: The American Period Room." *American Art Journal* 10, no. 1 (1978): 5–23.

Plummer Hall: Its Libraries, Its Collections, Its Historical Associations. Salem, MA: Salem Press, 1882.

"Salem, Massachusetts." 1911. Encyclopedia Brittanica Online, http://www.1911encyclopedia.org/Salem,_Massachusetts.

Whitehill, Walter Muir. *The East India Marine Society and the Peabody Museum of Salem; a Sesquicentennial History.* Salem, MA: Peabody Museum, 1949.

NEWSPAPERS AND DATABASES

Essex Register, January 1, 1827–December 31, 1827. Phillips Library, Salem, MA.

Impartial Register, May 12, 1800–December 1820. Salem Public Library, Salem, MA.

Salem Evening News, October 16, 1880–present. Salem Public Library, Salem, MA, and Phillips Library, MA.

Salem Gazette, October 18, 1781–February 6, 1786, Phillips Library, Salem, MA.

Salem Gazette, October 17, 1892-August 1909, Salem Public Library, Salem, MA.

Salem Mercury and *Salem Gazette*, 1786–1881. Phillips Library, Salem, MA.

Subject and biographical entries: Encyclopædia Britannica Online, Grove Music Online, and Gale Reference Groups.

About the Author

Maggi Smith-Dalton—singer and musician, independent scholar, historian, author, and educator—is a frequent lecturer on the integration of humanities and the arts and on American music and history. She has given lecture and performance programs at colleges and universities and in numerous professional-development courses for educators and teachers in all grade levels.

With her husband, she has researched and presented numerous public history courses, such as their popular American

Author Maggi Smith-Dalton. *Courtesy of Kevin Sparks.*

History Thru Music program that combines live performance and cultural history, since the 1980s. The Daltons also enjoy an active concert career.

She is founding president of the Salem History Society and cofounder and artistic director of the American History and Music Project at http://imhct.org.

Maggi authored a prize-winning short story and has been a lifelong history, cultural, arts and feature writer for newspapers and magazines.

Since 2006, she has written the history column "Naumkeag Notations" as well as arts and culture feature articles for the *Salem Gazette*.

Maggi produced a cable TV series and programmed and hosted musical theater, arts interviews and classical music shows for NPR, commercial, and community stations.

Visit us at
www.historypress.net